Human Rights

EQUALITY NOW

HUMAN RIGHTS

EQUALITY NOW

Safeguarding
Women's Rights

written by
Shirley Ann Wagner

Rourke Corporation, Inc.
Vero Beach, Florida 32964

Cover design: David Hundley

∞ The paper used in this book conforms to the American
National Standard for Permanence of Paper for Printed
Library Materials, Z39.48-1984.

Library of Congress Cataloging-in-Publication Data
Wagner, Shirley Ann, 1942-
    Equality now: safeguarding women's rights / by Shirley
Ann Wagner.
        p.   cm. — (Human rights)
    Includes bibliographical references and index.
    Summary: Discusses women's rights and the struggle to
secure them.
    ISBN 0-86593-177-1 (alk. paper)
    1. Women's rights — United States — Juvenile literature.
    2. Feminism — United States — Juvenile literature.
    [1. Women's rights. 2. Feminism.]   I. Title.   II.
Series: Human rights (Vero Beach, Fla.)
HQ1236.5.U6W34   1992   92-9746
305.42′0973 — dc20   CIP
                                                 AC

PRINTED IN THE UNITED STATES OF AMERICA

Contents

Human Rights

EQUALITY NOW

Chapter One

What Are Women's Rights?

We hold these truths to be self-evident: that all men are created equal, that they are endowed by their Creator with certain unalienable Rights, that among these are Life, Liberty and the pursuit of happiness. — That to secure these rights, Governments are instituted among Men, deriving their just powers from the consent of the governed. . . .
— THE DECLARATION OF INDEPENDENCE
OF THE UNITED STATES

The Declaration of Independence is one of the most important documents in United States history. In the Declaration, the founding fathers announced that they were becoming an independent nation, separating themselves from the government of England. They based their claims for independence on ideals not generally accepted at the time, that all *men* were created equal and that *men* had been given certain basic rights, including life, liberty, and the pursuit of happiness.

The Declaration of Independence was a revolutionary document for its time, but in one sense, it was not at all revolutionary. Women were not considered equal to men. Since women were not equal to men, they did not have the same God-given rights to life, liberty, and the pursuit of happiness. Government, established to protect the rights of men, did not protect the rights of women. Men could be governed only with their consent, while women could be governed without their consent. In a way, the Declaration of Independence established *inequality* for women in terms of rights. The history of women in the United States has often been a history of struggle to obtain the rights guaranteed to men.

The Declaration of Independence is housed with the Constitution and the Bill of Rights in the National Archives building. (National Archives)

Women and the Constitution

When the United States Constitution was written, it did little to improve the rights of women. The Constitution of the United States does not mention men or women. There are no statements that say that women cannot be president, senator, House representative, or Supreme Court justice. Nothing says that women will not be able to vote or to run for election. Nonetheless, the men who wrote the Constitution and the men who decided to adopt it as the new form of government imagined that men — those who owned property — would be the new voters. They also assumed that men would be the political leaders. The possibility of women having a role in the new government was not discussed at the Constitutional Convention.

State constitutions and state laws also did little to protect the rights of women. The United States Constitution gives states the power to make laws on their own. It specifically gives states the power to establish the conditions of *suffrage* (another word for voting rights). Most states established the qualifications for voters in their state constitutions or in state laws. The original voting laws of the states usually did not say that women could not vote. Most people simply assumed that women would not vote and did not have any reason to vote because men would take care of their needs.

Because women were not *explicitly* given equal rights in the national Constitution, in the state constitutions, or in state laws, women have challenged existing law, demanding that women be given equal rights.

Common Law

When the United States was developing as a nation, women were most directly affected by the laws passed by the state legislatures. Most state laws were based on English common law, which English settlers had brought with them to the

Colonies. Common law derives from customs and practices that have been followed in the past, rather than laws passed by the legislature. Judges examine each case that questions a common-law practice by comparing it to previous case decisions. That means that common law is difficult to change. Usually, changes occur only through the passage of new legislation. Under the common law, women had few rights. They were believed to need the protection of men, and men made all the significant decisions. Girls were under the protection of their fathers until they were married. Fathers made decisions for the entire family. After marriage, women were protected by their husbands, who made decisions for them. Women seldom had opportunities to make decisions for themselves.

When a woman married, she became legally a part of her husband. This system was known as *coverture*. Under this system, wives could not own property of their own, including their own clothing. If a married woman earned wages, that money belonged to her husband. A wife could not make contracts with other individuals. She usually needed her husband's permission to make her own last will and testament. Any property that a woman had owned prior to her marriage was managed by her husband. If a woman became unhappy with the way she was treated by her husband or with the way her husband used property that she had brought into the marriage, there was not much she could do to change her life. Divorce was seldom possible.

Under common law, single women actually had more legal rights than did married women. They were allowed to make contracts with other individuals, which meant that they could have businesses of their own. Single women could also sue and be sued, and they could make wills of their own. Few women, however, remained single. Families expected their daughters to marry. The daughters also expected themselves to marry and to have children. Many women married at a young age, moving from the father's to the husband's household. Few single women took full advantage of the few rights that were granted to them under common law.

Equal Rights vs. Protective Legislation

Often the rights for which women have fought have been rights men already had. Women have worked to be treated the same as men with regard to education, legal rights, voting rights, and employment rights. When they are asking for similar treatment, women argue that they are no different from men with respect to their need for these rights or their ability to make use of them. Women and men who believe that there are few important differences between men and women argue that men and women should have equal rights.

Not all demands for women's rights have been based on the equality of men and women. Some women and men have argued that women need special rights because of the ways that they are different from men. Between 1900 and 1920, many states passed laws that gave women rights that men did not have. These laws were known as *protective legislation.* State legislatures believed that such laws were needed because women were physically weaker than men or because women could bear children or were mothers. Some of the protective legislation that was passed was very helpful to women. For example, thirty-nine U.S. states passed laws that gave widows money to take care of their children.

Many women, as well as men, have fought for protective legislation for women. From the 1920's until the 1960's, many women's groups believed that protective legislation was more important for women than equal rights. These groups, such as the League of Women Voters, opposed an equal rights amendment to the Constitution because it would have made women equal to men, removing any legal grounds for legislation to protect women.

What Do Women Want?

The rights for which women in the United States have fought have included the rights mentioned in the Declaration of Independence: life, liberty, and the pursuit of happiness; equality; and the right to consent to be governed. Women have also fought to have the rights of citizens as defined in the United States and state constitutions, including the right to vote, the right to run for political office, the right to serve on juries, and the right to make legal contracts. Some of the rights for which women have fought were unique to their roles as wives and mothers. They have struggled to gain equal rights in employment and to have control over when they have children and how many children they have. In fighting for these rights, women attempted to change the common law that gave their fathers and husbands so much control over their lives.

Sometimes, as when they fought for protective legislation, women have argued for special rights for their special needs as women. Other times they have argued to be treated equally with men. While women's rights have increased throughout history, they still do not have all the rights and privileges of men. As long as this remains true, women will continue to fight for their rights.

Chapter Two

Movements
for
Women's Rights

Because women were excluded from political participation in the states and the nation, it was frequently difficult for them to get political leaders to pay attention to their issues or to pass laws related to their concerns. Women have been most successful at getting political and legal changes made when they have worked together in large groups or organizations. These groups have pressured lawmakers at the state and national levels to hear their demands. Twice in the history of the United States, these groups of women have become so large and so important that they became full-fledged social movements. Social movements occur when a broad-based group of individuals work together to achieve social and political change.

Two major social movements have worked for women's rights: the Women's Rights Movement and the Women's Liberation Movement. The Women's Rights Movement took place in the late nineteenth and early twentieth centuries. The Women's Liberation Movement, today known simply as the Women's Movement, developed in the late 1960's.

The Women's Rights Movement

In 1848, the first national women's rights convention was held in Seneca Falls, New York. Many of the women and men who attended this meeting were active in other reform movements of that time, particularly the Abolitionist Movement, which worked to free slaves and to treat them as human beings. As they looked at the treatment of slaves in the United States, these women began to notice similarities between their lives and those of the slaves: Both were denied the right to vote, to be fully educated, to make contracts, to earn and keep their own wages, to travel freely throughout the United States, or to sue individuals in a court of law. When they recognized these parallels, they became angry and began to fight for their own rights.

The women who attended the Seneca Falls convention drew up a list of grievances. This document was called the Declaration of Sentiments and was modeled on the Declaration of Independence. Like the Declaration of Independence, the Declaration of Sentiments listed the women's complaints about the ways they were treated; it also suggested solutions to the problems. The Declaration of Sentiments included statements about women's lack of *suffrage* (voting rights), their lack of legal rights (such as the right to make contracts or to sue individuals in a court of law), the subordination of women in the family, the inability of women to get an education equal to that offered to men, and the need for dress reform to allow greater freedom of movement for women than the clothes of the time made possible.

In the years before the Civil War, conventions on women's rights were held in many states. These groups attempted to get their state legislatures to pass laws or amendments to the state constitutions that would give women the right to vote. They also worked to educate people about other women's issues, including women's right to own property. Many of the well-known women in the nineteenth-century Women's Rights Movement were leaders at these state conventions: Susan B. Anthony, Elizabeth Cady Stanton, Lucy Stone, and Sojourner Truth were among them.

In the 1840's and 1850's, these women's groups were most successful at obtaining additional educational rights for women and gaining women's property rights. By 1860, many women were being trained as public school teachers, and some were also being trained as doctors. Married women's property reform laws passed in many states, giving wives the right to continue to own property after they married, the right to earn and keep their own wages, and rights to the custody of their children if their husbands left them or divorced them.

During the Civil War in the early 1860's, women temporarily set aside their demands to contribute to the war effort by

In 1920, the League of Women Voters was one of the first women's groups that fought for women's rights through the newly won right to vote. (Library of Congress)

performing jobs previously done by men. In both the North and the South, women managed the farms while men went off to fight the war. They also set up hospitals to care for the wounded. Large numbers of women were trained as nurses. Others organized supply deliveries to the soldiers. In Washington, D.C., several hundred women were trained as secretarial personnel to run the government agencies. As a result of their greater responsibilities during the Civil War, women gained confidence that they were politically as capable as men.

The end of the Civil War brought excitement. In 1865, the Thirteenth Amendment to the Constitution was passed, ending slavery in the United States. Women hoped that a constitutional amendment would be added to give voting rights to both former slaves and women. This did not occur. Instead, in 1868, the Fourteenth Amendment was passed. It was designed to expand the definition of U.S. citizenship and to extend the rights of citizenship.

The first section of this amendment provided a definition of citizenship that included "all persons born or naturalized in the United States," a phrase that clearly included women. However, the second section of the Fourteenth Amendment introduced the word "male" into the Constitution for the first time when it set up provisions for lowering the representation of any state that denied or abridged the right to vote in federal or state elections to "any of the *male* inhabitants of such State, being twenty-one years of age and citizens of the United States."

The Fifteenth Amendment was approved by the states in 1870, and it specifically gave voting rights to former slaves: "The right of citizens of the United States to vote shall not be denied or abridged by the United States or by any State on account of race, color, or previous condition of servitude. . . ." However, in light of the Fourteenth Amendment, it was believed to apply only to men who had been slaves.

Women were very angry, and as a result the Women's Rights Movement turned its attention to getting women the right to vote. For that reason, the first women's rights movement was known as the Woman Suffrage Movement. Unable to decide on a single strategy to accomplish this goal, the movement split into two groups in 1869. The National Woman Suffrage Association worked for an amendment to the United States Constitution, while the American Woman Suffrage Association worked at the state level to get amendments to the state constitutions to give women voting rights.

While the end of the Civil War did not automatically bring women the voting rights that they had hoped to gain, it did bring some successes for women that fostered the growth of the Women's Rights Movement in the long run. Opportunities for the education of women expanded. Separate colleges for women were opened in the eastern part of the United States, and some colleges in the West began to accept both men and women as students. College-trained women chose careers including law and religion. Additional organizations for women's rights were formed by African-American women, who unfortunately were often not accepted as equal participants in the white women's organizations. Black women initially worked for the right to vote and other legal rights without the help of white women.

By 1890, the Women's Rights Movement was focused on one goal: getting women the right to vote. The two national suffrage associations merged into one national organization, the National American Woman Suffrage Association (NAWSA). In 1920, their goal was achieved when the Nineteenth Amendment to the United States Constitution was passed. It reads, simply:

> The right of the citizens of the United States to vote shall not be denied or abridged by the United States or by any State on account of sex.

The successful achievement of the right to vote is usually seen as the end of the first women's movement. In the years to follow, a number of women's groups emerged and pursued a variety of different rights for women.

Women's groups continued to work for women's rights throughout the 1920's, the 1930's, the 1940's, and the 1950's. In the 1920's, for example, the Women's Joint Congressional Committee was formed to lobby Congress for laws of interest to women. Twenty-one different women's organizations were part of this joint committee in 1924. The lobbying efforts of these groups resulted in passage of two major pieces of legislation: the Sheppard-Towner Act, also known as the Maternity and Infancy Act of 1921, and the Cable Act of 1922. The Cable Act established individual citizenship for women, while the Sheppard-Towner Act provided money to states to improve prenatal care and infant hygiene.

In the 1930's, women's issues were championed by Eleanor Roosevelt, wife of President Franklin D. Roosevelt. Eleanor lobbied for women, trying to improve their position in the family and in the work force. She encouraged her husband to hire women as part of his administration. More women served in important government positions than ever before. Her daily newspaper column promoted women's issues. In 1933, she published a book entitled *It's Up to Women*, which encouraged women to meet the economic and political challenges of the time and assert themselves as leaders.

In the 1940's, growing numbers of women were drawn into the labor force because many men enlisted in the armed services or were drafted to fight in World War II. Women took jobs in areas that were once dominated by men: welding, riveting, factory work, sales, banking, and management. For the first time, women who were married were allowed to be schoolteachers and older women were allowed into the paid work force. They discovered that they were good at these jobs, so they remained in the work force after the war was over. Some stayed because they enjoyed the work. Others found it necessary to work to help support their families. By 1960, about 40 percent of women were employed, either full-time or part-time. About half of these women were mothers of children who were going to school. While many women and men continued to believe that women should work for wages only when they were single, women increasingly worked even when their children were attending school.

The New Women's Movement

In the 1960's, a broad-based movement for women's rights was again to emerge. Many people now believe that a primary cause for the development of the new movement was the growing gap between the "ideal" and the "real" woman's life. The ideal woman lived with her family until she became an adult. Then she either got married or worked in a "woman's job" (as a teacher, a secretary, a fashion model, or another "feminine" occupation) until she found "Mr. Right" and married him—usually by her early twenties. After they were married, women would stay at home and care for their husbands and children.

The popular culture of the 1950's had encouraged this image of women. Television, the new and increasingly popular medium, showed middle-class families such as the Cleavers in *Leave It to Beaver* or the Andersons in *Father Knows Best* in which Mother was always home, wearing a dress and heels and baking cookies or preparing a meal for her family when they returned home from school and work. Women's magazines such as *Ladies' Home Journal* and *Woman's Day*, sold in the grocery store, ran articles that warned women of psychological damage to children if their mothers worked outside the home. Films such as *Man of Distinction* depicted women who had to choose between successful careers and marriage. The clear message was that women could not have both a career and a family—and that women could not be truly happy unless they were married.

The modern women's rights movement has fought for passage of an Equal Rights Amendment. (Sally Ann Rogers)

This ideal image did not agree with the day-to-day realities faced by most women in the 1950's and 1960's. Throughout these decades, the number of married women who worked outside the home for wages kept increasing. Many women worked out of financial necessity — the money they earned was needed to support their families. Other women worked as a matter of choice — not only to earn money for themselves and their families but also to participate more fully in the world. As more women worked outside the home, they began to experience the ways in which they were treated differently from men. For example, women — regardless of their status or seniority — would be asked to make and serve coffee for visitors or meetings. Their bosses would refer to them as "girls," no matter how old they were. The inequities went beyond these social slights: In the 1970's, women in the workplace were paid only 59 cents for every dollar earned by a man; by 1990, that figure had risen to only 70 cents.

In 1961, President John F. Kennedy created the first President's Commission on the Status of Women. This group studied the social, legal, and political status of women in the United States and recommended new laws for Congress to pass. Commissions were also established in the states, to study inequities remaining in state laws. These commissions found that state laws often discriminated against women in education and employment, areas that were traditionally controlled by the states. While women's rights in these areas varied from state to state, in most states women were not treated as equal to men. Both Congress and the state legislatures were slow in reacting to the growing demand for women's rights. In 1966, a group of women formed the National Organization for Women (NOW). This organization began to identify women's issues that needed to be addressed. NOW was to become the most famous of a growing number of new women's organizations that would pressure Congress, the courts, and the state legislatures to improve rights for women.

At about the same time that NOW was emerging, women who had first worked in the Civil Rights Movement, which was concerned with increasing rights for black men and women, were focusing their attention on the unequal treatment of women.

This branch of the new women's movement was called the Women's Liberation Movement, and it is usually credited with inventing the "consciousness-raising" groups of the late 1960's and early 1970's. Consciousness-raising groups were small groups of women, often women who did not know one another. They met periodically to discuss the ways in which they were unfairly treated as women and to try to understand what caused this inequality.

Consciousness-raising groups and political organizations such as NOW helped women to define ways to gain equality. Through these groups, many women formed lasting friendships with other women, creating a sense of "sisterhood" that has lasted to this day, especially in the work world. Today, as a result of the movement in the 1960's and 1970's, many women "network" to help one another succeed in business and other endeavors.

The new women's movement has not always fully represented all the interests of the diverse cultures and populations of the United States. As a result, special women's organizations have developed to express the special concerns of women in these populations. For example, Native American women have built national organizations to address some issues specific to their lives. In 1978, a coalition known as Women of All Red Nations (WARN) met in Rapid City, South Dakota. More than thirty different native nations were represented at this conference. They identified a number of problems that Native American women faced, which were unfamiliar to white women.

Native American women had often been sterilized without their consent when they gave birth in hospitals attended by white doctors. Frequently, white social workers forced Native American women who were temporarily unable to care for their children to put the children up for adoption by white families. Native American women saw this as one of the ways that Native American families were destroyed by white laws. They also recognized that alcohol problems among Native Americans contributed to the difficulties of maintaining families, as had the historical losses of tribal lands and homes to the U.S. government in the nineteenth and twentieth centuries. In 1985, the Indigenous Women's Network, a group of Native American women, met and noted that many of these problems persisted.

Other groups of ethnic women developed organizations to consider how their problems were similar to or different from those of women in the United States as a whole: the National Black Feminists Organization, the Mexican American Women's National Association, the National Conference of Puerto Rican Women, and the Council of Jewish Women.

The Women's Liberation Movement that began in the 1960's is still alive today — although now, it is usually referred to simply as the Women's Movement. Throughout the 1970's, many people in the United States were aware of the Women's Movement and supported its goal of equality for women. Some people believe that the movement lost its effectiveness when it was unable to get the Equal Rights Amendment passed by the extended deadline of 1982 (see chapter 10). However, unlike the nineteenth-century movement, today's Women's Movement has given birth to many different political organizations and a variety of goals, not just political rights. If it is defeated on one issue, it will succeed with another.

Chapter Three

How Do Women Get Rights?

The organizations that women formed in the nineteenth and twentieth centuries have employed a variety of political tactics to press for women's rights. They have been faced with the task of convincing people who have political power — usually men — that women should have the same legal, political, or economic rights that men enjoy.

Legislatures

The primary method women have used to gain rights is to persuade legislators and voters to pass new laws. In the United States and Canada, laws can be passed at the local, state, or national level of government. Laws affecting women's rights have typically been passed by provincial or state legislatures or by the Canadian Parliament or the United States Congress. This means that the states or provinces have power to make laws on voting rights, marriage, divorce, and workers' rights. As a result, laws can vary widely from state to state or from province to province.

Every person needs to know what the law is, not only in her state but also in others that she might move to or visit. The nineteenth-century Women's Rights Movement based its organizing strategy on the fact that the most important laws affecting women's lives were made at the state level. Women organized state-by-state, because they knew that their state legislature, not the federal government, would have the greatest power over laws that directly affected them.

Because women could not vote in most states, they had to get men to vote for the rights of women. One way to do that was to *petition* the legislature. A petition is a formal request, usually addressed to a lawmaking body and signed by a group of people, which sets forth the signers' belief that a law should be made or changed, usually to guarantee a particular right. In a petition to a legislature, people sign their names to indicate that they agree with the petition's statement. Any group — even those who cannot vote — can write a petition and gather signatures to present to the legislature.

State legislatures change laws very slowly. During the time of the first Women's Rights Movement, lawmakers sometimes held sessions only once a year or once every two years. They were not available every day to discuss issues. By the late nineteenth century, women had begun to take their issues to the national legislatures — to the Congress in the United States or the Parliament in Canada — because the legislators in these national bodies were more available to listen to their concerns. They also recognized that if the national government passed a law, it would affect all the women in the country, not only the women in a particular state. Canadian women gained the right to vote in national elections through a national law.

The other advantage gained from focusing on the national legislature was that a smaller group of women could be organized in one place — such as Washington, D.C., or Ottawa — rather than having to maintain organizations everywhere. Women's groups in the nineteenth century began establishing offices in the capital cities and lobbying members of Congress or Parliament. They testified at public hearings in favor of particular laws. Most of the major women's organizations in the United States now have headquarters in Washington, D.C.

Since 1985, a growing number of national women's organizations have allied as a "Council of Presidents," meeting annually to establish a set of priorities for women's legislation known as the Women's Agenda (beginning in 1988). Having a set of priorities makes it easier for the women's groups to coordinate their lobbying efforts to focus on and achieve particular goals.

In addition, an effective lobbying group has developed within Congress. Since 1977, the Congressional Caucus for Women's Issues has introduced women's legislation each year and has lobbied for its passage. This caucus has more than one hundred members, men and women from both the Republican and Democratic parties. The congresswomen who are members of this group compose the Executive Committee and set the goals and priorities of the caucus in each legislative session. The Congressional Caucus has been successful in getting legislation passed that establishes pension rights for divorced

Legislation leads to opportunity, which leads to integration, which leads to acceptance, which leads to equality. The class of 1980 included the first woman to graduate from the Air Force Academy. (U.S. Department of Defense)

women and widows, gives housewives the right to have individual retirement accounts (IRAs), strengthens the payment of child support by allowing states to withhold past-due support from the father's wages, and provides funds for states to establish community-based child-care information and referral services. The Caucus has also sought the passage of other legislation: a Family and Medical Leave Bill for new parents, a child-care bill, bills to reduce infant mortality, and bills to give women economic equity.

Constitutional Amendments

To achieve rights, women have also used the process of amending state and national constitutions. The right to vote in all states was obtained by amending the Constitution in 1920 with the Nineteenth Amendment. In addition, fifteen states have passed equal rights amendments to their state constitutions: Alaska, Colorado, Connecticut, Hawaii, Illinois, Louisiana, Maryland, Massachusetts, Montana, New Hampshire, New Mexico, Pennsylvania, Texas, Virginia, and Washington. These amendments make explicit that women have the same rights as men in these states. The amendments serve as protection for women against the kind of discrimination that they faced in the past, when courts ruled that some rights applied only to men.

Many women would like to see an equal rights amendment added to the U.S. Constitution. Such an amendment would make it clear and beyond question that any law that applies to men applies equally to women.

Commissions on the Status of Women

Women can influence political decisions and raise women's issues to public attention by using the executive branch of government—that is, the president. For example, women can get the president to establish panels to examine issues and make recommendations for change. In 1961, President Kennedy was persuaded to appoint a President's Commission on the Status of Women. This group of thirteen women and eleven men presented a report, entitled *American Women*, to the president. The report supported the need for equal opportunity for women in education and in both full-time and part-time employment. It also argued that women should receive paid maternity leave and pointed out the need for adequate child care. The 1963 Equal Pay Act, which banned wage discrimination against women, is one result of the commission's work.

Succeeding presidents also established commissions on the status of women to examine the progress women were making in obtaining political, economic, and legal rights. Many states followed suit, focusing on the rights of women within the states. These groups have noted the similarity of women's problems across the states, and as a result new laws — at both the federal and state levels — have improved women's rights.

Civil Disobedience

Another tactic that women have used to make people aware of their rights is civil disobedience: the deliberate breaking of laws with the intention of making people aware of the unfairness of those laws. In the past, and even today, women have taken the risks of using this tactic in order to gain the rights denied to them. These women were willing to accept the penalties for their actions: arrest, fines, and even jail sentences.

The Case of Susan B. Anthony

A dramatic use of civil disobedience occurred in 1872. Women throughout the United States, who were angry that they had not received the right to vote along with black men, decided to attempt to vote in the 1872 presidential election. They actually *wanted* to be arrested for voting, so that they

One of the ways that women fight for their rights is through peaceful demonstration. (Paul Conklin/Uniphoto)

could challenge the constitutionality of the Fourteenth Amendment, which granted women citizenship but allowed them to be excluded from voting. In that way, they would be able to call the public's attention to the unfairness of their situation.

Susan B. Anthony, an activist and an organizer for the National Woman Suffrage Association, was one of the women who walked from her home to the voting poll in Rochester, New York, on the second Tuesday of November with the goal of being arrested. Anthony was allowed to vote, but two weeks later, she was arrested and brought to trial for having broken the state law, which was interpreted to allow only men to vote. She attempted to convince the judge that he should interpret the Fourteenth Amendment liberally: She should have the right to vote because, she claimed, she was a citizen and all citizens were supposed to have equal rights. If only men were allowed to vote, she, *a citizen*, was being treated unequally. In particular, Anthony tried to get the judge to agree that she, and other women, had the right to choose the people who represented them in government.

Anthony was found guilty and was fined $100. She refused to pay her fine, hoping that the judge would put her in jail. Instead, the judge never demanded that the fine be paid. As a result, Anthony's case went no further than her local court, and her ultimate goal of testing the Constitution was unsuccessful.

The National Woman's Party

Since 1916, some women have believed that they can be most effective if they have a separate women's political party. The National Woman's Party (NWP) was founded by Alice Paul and Lucy Burns. These women organized women in the twelve states where women, at that time, had the right to vote in presidential elections. Then, the NWP ran its own candidates for the presidency and Congress.

In 1917, the NWP used some of the tactics that had been used by British suffragettes to bring attention to their demand for voting rights. They marched in Washington, D.C., during the inauguration ceremony for President Woodrow Wilson. They picketed the White House and Congress, marching back and forth with signs. When the police were called to arrest them, some of the picketers chained themselves to the fences. In jail, some went on hunger strikes. All of these tactics attracted the attention of newspapers and other media. Many people were angry with the way that the women were treated and urged the president and Congress to meet their demands. Today, some historians believe that the NWP's tactics were crucial to the passage of the Nineteenth Amendment. Later organizations adopted the NWP's approach, influencing elections and the selection of candidates who would support women's issues. These organizations include the National Women's Political Caucus, founded in 1971, and the Council of Presidents, which established its Women's Agenda in 1988.

Throughout history, women have used a variety of strategies to fight for their rights. Whenever one tactic lost its effectiveness, they tried new ones or returned to tactics that had worked in the past. In each area where women have gained rights, some methods have been more effective than others.

Chapter Four

Voting Rights

Voting is the most essential political right in democracies and is recognized as a fundamental right in the United Nations' Universal Declaration of Human Rights (1948). Voting allows people to participate in the selection of their leaders. In democracies such as the United States and Canada, government officials at the local, state or provincial, and national levels are chosen by citizens who vote.

Throughout history, women have often been excluded from voting. In countries throughout the world, they have had to organize to obtain voting rights. Some people are surprised to learn, for example, that women in Switzerland did not gain the right to vote until 1971.

Voting Rights in the United States

In the United States Constitution, each state was given the power to determine who was eligible to vote. In the 1790's, when the nation was new, state constitutions and laws seldom denied women the right to vote *explicitly*. In fact, the constitutions did not mention gender qualifications for voting. However, since most of the states gave voting rights to property owners, and since few women had the right to own property, the general assumption was that women would not vote.

New Jersey: An Exception to the Rule

In the state of New Jersey, the 1776 New Jersey constitution gave the vote to "all inhabitants" who met specified property and residency requirements. No restrictions against voting were placed upon women who met these property and residence requirements. In this way, the New Jersey constitution was similar to the constitutions and laws of the other thirteen states, which also did not explicitly prohibit women from voting.

What was different about New Jersey was that, when the legislature revised its election law in 1790, it used the phrase *he or she* when referring to eligible voters. Under this law, women in seven of New Jersey's thirteen counties were allowed to vote if they met the property and residency qualifications. A revision of the 1790 law gave voting rights to women in the other six counties.

It is not easy to determine how many women actually voted in the elections held in New Jersey, because few voting records for that time period still exist. However, in 1807, the New Jersey legislature revoked women's right to vote. The legislature passed a law that restricted the right to vote to white male citizens who were twenty-one years of age or older. With this law, New Jersey's legislators *disenfranchised* — that is, took the vote away from — women, free blacks (both male and female), and non-citizens. All of these people had previously had the right to vote. It was not until 1920, with the passage of the Nineteenth Amendment to the U.S. Constitution, that women in New Jersey would again be allowed to vote.

Organizing to Get the Vote

New Jersey's disenfranchisement of women voters was reflected across the states. During the early nineteenth century, many states added the words "white men" to the state laws on suffrage. Women challenged these laws in a number of ways.

In the 1872 presidential election, many women, just like Susan B. Anthony, attempted to vote. When they did so, they knew that they might be arrested and thrown into jail, but they did not mind. They hoped that, in this way, they could take their cases directly to the United States Supreme Court, where they would challenge the laws that denied their right to vote. This tactic did not work quite as well as the women had hoped. In some communities, women were allowed to cast their ballots. In others, they were arrested and sometimes fined or sent to jail. Often they were pardoned or the charges against them were dropped, so that they could not appeal the court decisions to the Supreme Court.

In 1875, the Supreme Court finally considered the question of whether women had the constitutional right to vote. In the case of *Minor v. Happersett*, Virginia Minor's husband sued on her behalf, because under common law, she could not sue for herself. The court, in its decision, said that women were both state citizens and national citizens. However, the United States Constitution did not define citizenship to include voting rights. This meant that the decision about whether women had voting rights was left to the states. In effect, the Supreme Court ruled

In a 1912 demonstration for the right to vote, women young and old, black and white march in New York. (Library of Congress)

against women's right to vote.

Shortly before the decision in *Minor v. Heppersett*, the American Woman Suffrage Association (AWSA) and the National Woman Suffrage Association (NWSA) had been founded. These two women's suffrage organizations were active between 1870 and 1890, and they agreed that women should be given the right to vote. They disagreed, however, about the strategies that should be used to obtain the vote for women. The NWSA favored working for an amendment to the United States Constitution to give women voting rights. The AWSA believed that voting rights could be most successfully obtained state by state.

The strategy of attempting to gain the right to vote state by state made for slow progress. Some states were willing to grant women limited suffrage rights, limiting voting to school elections or tax and bond elections. Sometimes women in cities were given the right to vote in municipal elections. Several states gave women the right to vote in presidential elections or primaries. In only fifteen states did women have full suffrage rights.

In 1890, the AWSA and the NWSA united as the National American Woman Suffrage Association (NAWSA), with the sole purpose of securing for women the right to vote. The merger of these two groups focused women's efforts on getting Congress to pass a constitutional amendment to give women voting rights. It took twenty-nine years of lobbying members of Congress before this goal was finally achieved. In 1919, an amendment to the United States Constitution was passed by Congress and was sent to the states for ratification. In 1920, the Nineteenth Amendment was ratified in time for women to be able to vote in that year's presidential election.

The Nineteenth Amendment

While the Nineteenth Amendment appeared to grant voting rights to all women, in reality it secured this right primarily for white women. The amendment intended for black women to be included as well. However, most Southern states had passed laws in the nineteenth century that made it extremely difficult for black men and black women to participate as voters. Sometimes these laws required those who wished to vote to pay a poll tax (a fee) before they could register to vote. Some laws required people to pass literacy tests before they could register; these tests naturally discriminated against voters who were unable to read. Other laws said that new voters could register to vote only if their grandfathers had had the right to vote. Because many of the grandparents of black men and women had been slaves, such laws barred them from voting. When laws failed to discourage blacks from registering to vote, violence might also be used against them. All of these tactics made it difficult, if not impossible, for African Americans in many states to have any say in who would make the laws and who would govern at the local, state, and national levels.

It was not until 1965 that Congress passed the Voting Rights Act. This law made many of the discriminatory voting practices of the Southern states illegal. It also allowed federal officials to register black voters, which helped to remove the threat of violence when blacks attempted to register. This made it possible for black women to participate fully as voters.

Native American women were also not automatically included as voters after the passage of the Nineteenth Amendment. Earlier court cases had determined that Native American men who lived on reservations could not vote because they did not pay taxes. In 1924, Congress passed a law that extended voting rights to Native American men and women.

The Voting Rights Act of 1970 made the age for voting the same from state to state by extending the right to vote to all men and women over the age of eighteen. The Twenty-sixth Amendment to the Constitution solidified this right.

Voting Rights in Canada

Women in Canada tried many of the same strategies used by women in the United States to obtain the right to vote. Canada has a federal system of government with a combination of national, provincial, and local elections. Women in Canada had to win the right to vote province by province. By 1900, Euroamerican women who owned property could vote in municipal elections in all provinces except Quebec, which had allowed women who owned property to vote between 1809 and 1849 but had removed this right in 1850. On May 24, 1918, all Euroamerican female citizens who were twenty-one years of age or older were given the right to vote in national elections. Euroamerican women in the provinces of New Brunswick, Prince Edward Island, Newfoundland, and Quebec were not allowed to vote in provincial elections or to run for political office, even though they could vote in the national elections. Gradually, each province gave these women the right to vote in provincial elections. Quebec was the last province to grant this right; it did so in 1940.

Like their sisters in the United States, Native American women in Canada were the last group of women to achieve voting rights. For them, this right did not come until 1960.

International Voting Rights

Internationally, New Zealand was the first country to grant women the right to vote, in 1893. Australia, Finland, Russia, Denmark, Iceland, Canada, Sweden, and Austria all granted women the right to vote before the United States did. Most nations, however, gave women the right to vote after 1920.

The Gender Gap

In the past, women have been slow to exercise their legal right to vote, but that has changed as women have become more economically active in the work force. In the United

When Did Women Get the Vote?
Selected Countries

By Year		By Nation	
1893	New Zealand	Argentina	1947
1902	Australia	Australia	1902
1906	Finland	Austria	1919
1914	Russia	Belgium	1948
1915	Denmark	Brazil	1932
1915	Iceland	Canada	1918
1918	Canada	China	1949
1919	Sweden	Colombia	1954
1919	Austria	Denmark	1915
1920	United States	Egypt	1956
1921	Norway	Finland	1906
1922	Netherlands	France	1945
1928	Great Britain	Ghana	1950
1931	Spain	Great Britain	1928
1932	Brazil	Iceland	1915
1945	France	India	1950
1946	Italy	Italy	1946
1946	Japan	Japan	1946
1946	Venezuela	Korea	1948
1947	Argentina	Lebanon	1953
1948	Belgium	Mexico	1953
1948	Korea	Netherlands	1922
1949	China	New Zealand	1893
1950	India	Nigeria	1977
1950	Ghana	Norway	1921
1953	Lebanon	Russia	1914
1953	Mexico	Spain	1931
1954	Colombia	Sudan	1964
1956	Egypt	Sweden	1919
1964	Sudan	Switzerland	1971
1971	Switzerland	United States	1920
1977	Nigeria	Venezuela	1946

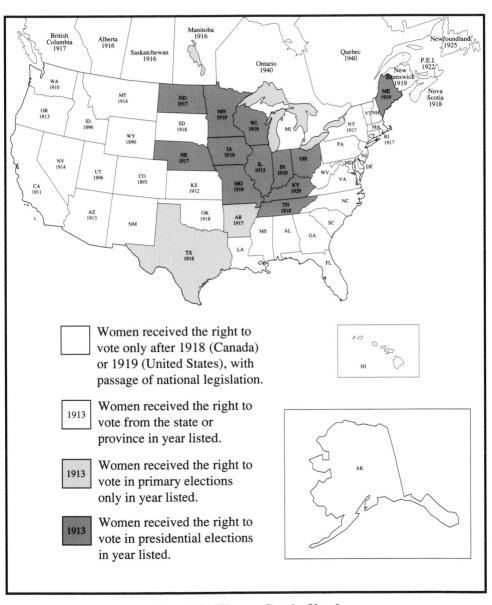

Women received the right to vote only after 1918 (Canada) or 1919 (United States), with passage of national legislation.

1913 Women received the right to vote from the state or province in year listed.

1913 Women received the right to vote in primary elections only in year listed.

1913 Women received the right to vote in presidential elections in year listed.

When Did Women Get the Vote?

States, while data on voting are not very reliable until the 1960's, it is clear that smaller percentages of women than men turned out to vote in local, state, and national elections until the 1970's. What was more surprising to people, however, was that when women did vote, they did not appear to make voting decisions any differently from men voters.

However, as the turnout of women has increased, some important differences have emerged between women and men on political issues. These differences are being characterized by the media as a "gender gap." In the 1980, 1984, and 1988 U.S. presidential elections, the gender gap was visible and growing. This gap is apparent in all age groups of women, although it is most pronounced among women under age sixty. It also cuts across racial, socioeconomic, and regional differences.

The impact of the gender gap on elections is not yet clearly defined, but it is fair to say that many politicians now believe that they must speak to issues that are seen as women's issues and must attempt to win women voters if they are to gain office. Women voters, therefore, are being taken more seriously as a political force. More than half a century after achieving the right to vote, women are beginning to use that right as a political tool.

	Percentage of Voter Turnout in Presidential Elections				
	1972	1976	1980	1984	1988
Men	64.1	59.6	59.1	59.0	56.4
Women	62.0	58.8	59.4	60.8	58.3

SOURCE: U.S. Bureau of the Census, *Statistical Abstract of the United States, 1988.*

Chapter Five

Political and Legal Rights

The right to vote is the single most significant political right in a free society, because it gives people the power to participate in the selection of their leaders. Often, it also gives them the right to run for political office and become political leaders themselves. However, to be full participants in their society, the citizens of a democracy must fulfill other political rights and obligations. In the United States, even after women obtained the right to vote, they were sometimes excused from these obligations — and denied the corresponding rights.

The Right and Obligation to Serve on Juries

In democratic societies such as Canada and the United States, anyone accused of having committed a crime has a right to trial by a jury of his or her peers. These peers should represent a cross-section of the population, including individuals from all occupations, classes, and ethnic groups.

Just as women were once denied the right to vote, they were once excluded from serving on juries. States gave many reasons for excluding women from juries: They said that women's duties as homemakers were too important to release them for jury duty; that women might have to listen to disagreeable evidence that might offend them; and that women serving on juries might have to be sequestered overnight, which would keep them from their families. In other words, women were denied the same duties and rights as men, all in the name of "protecting" them. Such protections assumed that adult women were different from adult men — that they were more vulnerable and therefore in need of such protection.

In 1948 in the United States, only twenty-eight states called for women to serve on juries. Even in those states, women could frequently refuse to serve without giving any reason for their refusal. Men, on the other hand, were expected to serve when called. In 1961, a woman in Florida challenged the state's jury selection process. Florida did allow women to serve on juries but made the process for women's selection difficult, and few women were actually chosen for jury service. The woman who brought the lawsuit against Florida's law was named Hoyt. She had been convicted by an all-male jury of murdering her husband. Her lawyers believed that she needed women on the jury to get a fair trial. The Supreme Court disagreed and upheld the constitutionality of the Florida law on the grounds that women could still be "protected" from some processes of community and political life.

In 1970, the Supreme Court changed its mind in *Taylor v. Louisiana*. Taylor was a man who had been convicted by an all-male jury. His lawyers said that a fair jury should be a cross-sample of all people in the community. This time the Supreme Court agreed that state laws which excluded women from juries were unconstitutional. In 1979, the Supreme Court went even further. In *Duren v. Missouri*, the court decided that state laws regarding jury service must treat men and women the same. State laws that allowed women to choose not to serve on juries were therefore unconstitutional.

Today, women's names are selected for jury duty in the same random process that is used to select male jurors, regardless of the state. As a result, women are fulfilling another of the key obligations of citizenship in a democratic society.

Marriage Laws

During the fifty years that women were organizing to get the right to vote, they were also actively working to improve

Women and African Americans did not serve on juries in the early twentieth century;
pictured is the jury for the Scopes trial. (Library of Congress)

other rights for women. Some of the rights that concerned
women most related to marriage, divorce, and child custody.

Under common law, marriage was a contract based on the
mutual consent of the man and woman. Once married,
however, the husband and wife were legally treated as a single
person — represented by the husband. A woman took her
husband's name, and the husband made all the important
decisions, including where they would live. All property was
under the management of the husband, even that which the
wife owned prior to the marriage. One of the woman's only
protections was that the husband had to leave at least one-third
of their property to her if he died before she did.

In the United States, each state — and in Canada, each
province — determines its own laws regarding marriage. In the
nineteenth century, the law varied considerably from one state
or province to the next. In some states and provinces, not all
women had the legal right to marry. While men and women
who were slaves often married, their marriages had no legal
status. Their owner could sell either one of them and break up

the marriage. He also could sell any of the children born to the couple.

In the middle of the nineteenth century, states began to pass laws to protect women's rights to own property even after they were married. Mississippi was the first state to pass a Married Women's Property Act, in 1839. By 1865, twenty-nine states had such laws, which allowed women to continue to own the property that they had owned prior to the marriage or property that they received after marriage as gifts or bequests from family members.

Some states developed their marital property laws from Spanish law rather than common law. According to Spanish law, women retained some rights to property after marriage. These states were called community-property states because the husband and wife were seen as owning all property in marriage jointly. Community-property states, however, allowed husbands complete management of all jointly owned property. Husbands did need the consent of their wives to sell the property. Reform in community-property states moved toward giving women the right to manage their own property. One reason that married women's property acts were passed in a number of states is that men in state legislatures were willing to support them. Often, men voted for these laws because they had been the fathers or brothers of women whose husbands had lost or gambled away the property or wages that their wives had earned.

In the twentieth century, marriage laws became similar from state to state. Many states have passed a Uniform Pre-marital Agreement Act, which allows men and women to make agreements, prior to marriage, about how they will divide their property if they divorce. According to such laws, a woman can either retain her maiden name when she marries or take her husband's name — or both the husband and the wife can use a combination of their names.

Divorce

Divorce is a legal way of ending a marriage between a man and a woman. Many countries have made it difficult for men and women to divorce legally, by restricting the reasons that can be used to end a marriage. Often, the reasons given for such restrictions have been religious: Marriage, according to many religions, is viewed as a sacred covenant between a man and a woman and should not be ended except by the death of the husband or wife.

In the United States and Canada, divorce laws are established by the states and provinces. As each state defined marriage, it also defined the conditions under which marriage could be ended. Initially, the states mainly followed English common law, which usually prevented "absolute divorce" (a complete ending of the marriage which allowed each individual to remarry). Common law did allow for a legal separation of husbands and wives in situations of adultery, desertion, or cruelty. In a legal separation, husbands and wives could maintain separate households, but neither could remarry. If the husband was the person who had committed the adultery or cruelty or had deserted his wife, he could also be ordered to pay money to support his former wife and their children.

The colonies established on the American continent followed the common-law practice of allowing only for legal separations. Some colonies, such as Connecticut and Massachusetts, did allow for absolute divorces. After the American Revolution, some states enacted divorce laws, while others retained only legal separations. At the Seneca Falls convention in 1848, the rights of women to divorce, to gain custody of their children, and to retain a share of the property after divorce were among the rights women wanted to secure. Each state determined its own divorce laws, and these laws varied from state to state, but most states made divorces difficult to obtain.

In the 1960's, the Women's Liberation Movement stressed the need to improve the divorce laws. In the 1970's, many states enacted "no-fault" divorce laws. The phrase *no-fault* meant that a divorce could be granted to individuals without a court battle in which one person had to prove that he or she had been wronged by the other. In no-fault divorces, either the husband or the wife has the right to request a divorce from the other.

There is some evidence that no-fault divorces, while they give greater equality to women to initiate divorce proceedings, may be harmful to women economically. In no-fault divorces, women generally receive lower sums of money to support themselves (alimony) and lower amounts of money to support their children (child support). Because women continue to earn less in wages than men earn, the "equal treatment" of a no-fault divorce may, in reality, be unfair to the mothers and children of these divorced families.

Child Custody

An issue closely related to divorce is who gets custody of the children if a marriage ends. Under common law, the children were considered the absolute property of the husband. It was not until the 1850's that many states passed laws which established the rights of mothers to the custody of their children. Their rights were never absolute, since most state laws left the decision about who should have the custody of the children to the courts.

Many of these courts followed an idea found in a New Jersey law of 1860. This law said that infants, children under the age of puberty, and children with any kind of health problem should be placed in the custody of the mother when there was a divorce, unless the mother was judged to be unfit to care for the children. Laws such as the one in New Jersey frequently forced women to fight for the custody of their children when they went through a divorce. Often, if the woman had committed adultery or deserted her husband, she was automatically judged to be unfit to have custody of the children.

The reemergence of the women's movement a century later generated new discussion about child custody decisions. The movement was based on a notion of equal rights for both men and women. In the area of child custody, men were often treated as having fewer rights than women. Discussions of child custody began to focus on what was in the best interests of the father, the mother, and each child.

Increasingly, fathers are fighting to establish that they are equally willing to care for their children and should have equal rights to custody in case of a divorce. Some states have passed laws that allow the option of joint custody, where each parent retains rights to share in the rearing of the children. In some situations, children are consulted by the judge making the custody decision. In other cases, social workers attempt to determine which parent can better provide for the needs of the children once there is a divorce.

Credit

When husbands were considered the primary heads of household, they were considered responsible for the financial needs of the family. Women were unable to get loans or have credit cards without the approval of their husbands. In 1975, Congress passed the Equal Credit Opportunity Act, which allowed married and single women to get loans and credit cards in their own names.

While this law made it easier for women to get personal credit, they still experienced difficulty getting the larger commercial loans necessary to establish businesses. In 1988, the Women's Business Ownership Act was passed by Congress. This law prohibits discrimination against women who want business loans.

Chapter Six

Reproductive Rights

Throughout history, people in all societies have attempted to control the number of children that women have. Sometimes, societies have wanted women to have fewer children because the population was already large and difficult to feed. At the same time, some women have had an interest in preventing pregnancy in order to limit the number of children they had. When countries are interested in limiting the size of their population, they usually make it easy for women to have access to information and products that will help them prevent pregnancy. At other times, they have made it illegal for women to obtain different methods of birth control. This has led women to organize to try to gain *reproductive rights*: rights to maintain control over their own bodies and their decisions to give birth to children.

Birth Control

"Birth control" refers to all methods of preventing pregnancy, but in contemporary times, birth control most frequently refers to the use of contraceptives: devices that prevent women from getting pregnant while allowing them to engage in sexual relationships. Some form of birth control has been practiced since ancient times. Women have had to find some way of controlling their pregnancies for a wide variety of reasons—from economic need to their own health safety. The risks of childbirth were once great and even today can threaten a woman's health in some cases. Repeated or constant pregnancies forced women to remain economically dependent on men and, at worst, placed them in fear for their lives.

In the early twentieth century, Margaret Sanger organized women in the United States to try to legalize the distribution of contraceptives that were then available in Europe. Sanger was arrested for establishing a clinic that distributed information about birth control and provided contraceptives to women. By the 1920's, some states were allowing married women to obtain prescriptions for contraceptives from their doctors. This gave women more control than they had had in the past over whether they became pregnant. Other states continued to prohibit the prescription, sale, and use of contraceptives. Connecticut was one of the states that had such a law. In 1965, in *Griswold v. Connecticut*, the Supreme Court decided that Connecticut's law was unconstitutional because it restricted the sale and use of contraceptive devices, even to married couples. In 1972, however, the Court made it illegal for unmarried

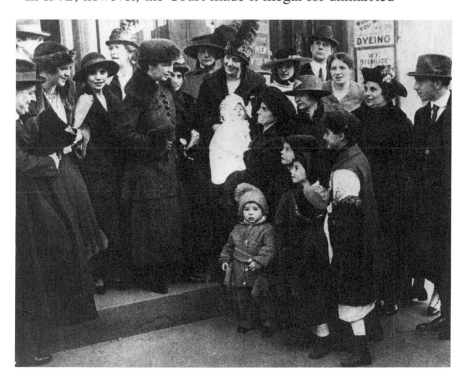

At a birth control trial in New York City, several poor mothers brought their large families to aid Margaret Sanger in court. (Library of Congress)

people to use and purchase contraceptives.

Even though some kinds of contraceptives are now easy to obtain in the United States, in the 1980's and 1990's, women have had to organize to try to obtain some of the newer contraceptives that have been developed in other countries. China, which is using a number of measures to keep births down, has pioneered several new methods, one of which is a birth control pill that men take. France has also developed a number of new methods, including a contraceptive that can be implanted under the skin and is believed to be highly effective.

Many have debated over whether birth control information should be available to teenagers. Some schools now provide students with information about contraceptives, such as condoms, because they know that there are large numbers of teenage girls who get pregnant and are faced with the difficulties of becoming mothers before they are fully able to take care of themselves. Schools have also become concerned about actually making the contraceptives themselves available to the students, because some forms of contraceptives can help prevent people from getting acquired immune deficiency syndrome (AIDS). As the AIDS epidemic increases, there will be more pressure to make contraceptives available to both men and women to help prevent the spread of this fatal disease.

Abortion

Women have also organized to gain and keep the right to abortion. In medical terms, abortion is the termination of a pregnancy, and it may be either spontaneous or induced. If an abortion is spontaneous, the woman's body rejects the pregnancy naturally. Many pregnancies end in this manner for reasons that doctors do not fully understand. Spontaneous abortions are considered nature's way of letting the woman's body know that the pregnancy is not healthy. An induced abortion, on the other hand, is one caused by an outside medical procedure, or "intervention," to terminate the pregnancy. When people use the term "abortion," they are usually referring to induced abortion.

As one form of birth control, abortion has been practiced in most societies. Controversy surrounding the use of abortions is long-standing. Ancient Greek physicians, for example, agreed not to perform abortions. In the United States, abortion was legal until the latter part of the nineteenth century. Physicians and midwives performed abortions for pregnant women who requested them prior to the point in pregnancy that is referred to as "quickening," when the woman can feel the fetus move. Quickening usually takes place between twelve and fourteen weeks after the woman becomes pregnant.

Having an abortion prior to quickening was not seen as illegal or sinful in most parts of the United States until sometime between the 1860's and the 1880's. During that time, male physicians organized to prevent midwives — women who treated expectant mothers during pregnancy, delivered their babies, and provided them with natural methods of birth control and abortion — from being able to practice. These doctors persuaded state legislatures to pass laws to make abortions illegal. In 1821, Connecticut was the first state to pass a law that made it illegal for women to obtain an abortion and for doctors or other individuals to perform abortions. By 1860, twenty states had laws that restricted abortion. Because these laws lasted for more than one hundred years, many people came to believe that abortions had always been illegal in the United States. In 1965, all fifty states had anti-abortion laws, although some states did allow abortions to be performed if the mother's life were endangered by the pregnancy.

One of the things that the Women's Liberation Movement made clear during the 1960's was that, even when abortions were illegal, many women still used abortion as a means of birth control. Wealthy women were able to go to other countries where abortions were legal and have medically safe abortions. Poor women often attempted to induce abortion by themselves, or they had illegal abortions in medically unsafe conditions. Often women developed infections or bled profusely from botched abortions; sometimes they died.

The Women's Liberation Movement pressed states to make changes in their abortion laws. Initially, this meant that the laws expanded the reasons that women could seek abortions, adding rape, incest, threat to the mother's life, and occasionally fetal deformity. These laws, however, continued to treat the woman as someone who needed the permission of another adult to make a decision to have an abortion. Frequently, women needed the consent of their husband if they were married or of their parents if they were not. The consent of a doctor was also necessary.

In the late 1960's and early 1970's, women increasingly took their reproductive issues to the Supreme Court. In 1973, the Supreme Court, in a landmark case known as *Roe v. Wade*,

Pro-choice and pro-life activists demonstrate. (Grant/PhotoBank)

ruled that state laws which banned abortions in the first twelve weeks of pregnancy were unconstitutional. The woman in this case, identified as Jane Roe (a pseudonym to protect her real identity), had become pregnant against her will when she was raped. She wanted to have an abortion in Texas. However, Texas allowed women to have abortions only if necessary to save the life of the mother. With the encouragement of women's rights lawyers, she brought her case to the Supreme Court to challenge the constitutionality of the Texas state law. Roe was not allowed an abortion. In fact, her case arrived at the Supreme Court after she had already given birth. Nevertheless, the Court finally decided that Roe should have been allowed to have an abortion. Because of this ruling, women in many parts of the United States were able to obtain medically safe abortions, after consultation with a physician.

The *Roe v. Wade* decision is one of the most controversial decisions the Supreme Court has ever made. The judges quickly discovered that making one decision about abortion was not the end of their work but only the beginning. In the years since *Roe*, the court has decided a number of other abortion cases. Many of their later decisions have restricted the access of women to abortion as a method of terminating pregnancy.

One of the most significant restrictions on abortion came in a 1980 case, *Harris v. McRae*. The Supreme Court decided that federal legislation prevented the use of federal Medicaid money for abortion unless the mother's life were endangered or the pregnancy were the result of rape or incest. For many poor women, this decision again meant that abortions were not available to them because of cost.

As of the early 1990's, Alaska, California, Connecticut, Delaware, Hawaii, Maryland, Massachusetts, New Jersey, New York, North Carolina, Oregon, Vermont, Washington, and West Virginia still supported public aid for poor women who want abortions for a wide range of reasons. Other states, however, follow the guidelines established by *Harris v. McRae*.

Pro-Choice and Pro-Life Arguments

The women's groups that championed the drive for abortion rights in the state legislatures and the nation's courts are often called "pro-choice," because they believe that the choice about whether to terminate a pregnancy belongs to the woman, since it is her body that houses the child until birth. This group argues that abortion should be determined by the woman in consultation with her physician and her own conscience — that the decision on whether to have an abortion cannot be dictated by government, since government cannot take into account all individual circumstances and should not dictate individual choice. Those in the pro-choice camp also believe that abortion should be one method available to women who wish to control their pregnancies. They believe that abortion will be necessary as long as contraceptives cannot fully guarantee the prevention of pregnancy. Women, they believe, should have full control over their own bodies.

Even women who agree on the need for abortion as one option for terminating pregnancy may disagree on how far into the pregnancy an abortion should occur. For many people, the central question is: When does life begin? Pro-life groups, which since the 1980's have organized to overturn legal abortions, believe that the life of the unborn child begins at the second in time when a woman becomes pregnant: at conception. Others argue that life begins when a child is born. Still others believe that life begins when the fetus, the unborn child, is "viable" — that is, when it can live and grow outside the mother's body by itself or on supportive machines.

From the pro-life perspective, the life of the unborn child is as important as the life of the mother. Since pro-life adherents believe that the life of the unborn child begins at conception,

The Pregnancy Discrimination Act of 1978 prohibits discrimination against women because of pregnancy. (Julie Marcotte/Uniphoto)

they believe that the government should protect the life of the unborn child throughout a pregnancy. Some pro-life people would protect the life of the child regardless of the circumstances under which a woman became pregnant, even if she had been raped. Others would allow abortion in cases of rape or incest or if the life of the mother were endangered.

Women are organized on both sides of the abortion issue. In the United States, the major organization for women who favor abortion is the National Abortion Rights Action League (NARAL). The major organization for those opposed to abortion is the National Right to Life Committee.

Sterilization

Another issue in reproductive rights is sterilization. Sterilization is a permanent form of birth control. When a man is sterilized, he loses the ability to make a woman pregnant. When a woman is sterilized, she loses the ability to become pregnant and have children. Men and women can choose to be sterilized through "voluntary sterilization."

Sometimes either men or women have been sterilized against their will or even without their knowledge. The Women's Liberation Movement in the 1960's brought to public attention the fact that poor women, particularly minority women such as African-American women, Puerto Rican women, and Native American women, were frequently sterilized without being fully informed of the consequences of these procedures. In 1974, the U.S. Department of Health, Education, and Welfare issued guidelines that required sterilization to be truly voluntary, informed, and competent.

Chapter Seven

Employment Rights

Women throughout the world make important contributions to the economics of their countries. Often, their work is not fully recognized because it occurs within the home and family. They prepare food and do housework. They tend children. They may grow and preserve fruits and vegetables for their family's use. They may make clothing for their family members. When family members are ill, women often care for them until they are well again. Most societies treat all this work as unpaid labor. When people speak of women's *employment* rights, they are referring to their work as members of the labor force, for which they receive wages or salaries.

In contemporary society, increasing percentages of women in every society have joined this work force, so employment rights are becoming more significant as women's issues. Women who work outside the home do so for the same reasons as men: They need the money to support themselves and their families. In the past, since men have traditionally been seen as the major breadwinners for their families, employers have considered it acceptable to pay them higher wages.

When women began working outside the home, they worked during the years before they were married, stayed at home while they were rearing their families, and perhaps returned to the workplace after their children were grown. Of course, some women, particularly those who had low incomes, had to continue to work even when they had families. People ignored the gap between this reality and the ideal image that women

In 1905, it was not unusual for women to work in crowded sweatshops.
(Collection of Deborah Cooney)

could be supported by their fathers or husbands. About 25 percent of women worked outside the home as early as the 1920's.

A large expansion of women in the work force occurred in the 1940's, during World War II, when women held jobs that had previously been done only by men. In the 1950's, while the media attempted to romanticize the role of the housewife and mother, many women found that these roles were not totally fulfilling, and they returned to work at part-time jobs, when their children were in school. A growing number of women also found that it was necessary to work outside the home to help support their families. Each decade — the 1960's, the 1970's, the 1980's, and the 1990's — has seen a steady growth in the number of women employed outside the home.

As women's participation in the work force has expanded, the demand for rights for women workers has increased. Typically, these demands have focused on two key issues: gaining access to jobs that have previously been considered for men only, and improving the wages of women who are employed.

Protective Legislation

In the nineteenth century, most women saw protective legislation as the most important way to obtain employment rights. Protective legislation attempted to limit the hours that men, women, and children could work and the minimum wages that they could be paid. Courts struck down these laws as unconstitutional when applied to men. However, judges were more sympathetic to the arguments that women and children needed special protection because they were physically weaker than men. Women were also seen as needing special protection because they were the childbearers.

By 1900, many states had passed protective legislation for women workers. Usually, these laws limited the number of hours that women could work and prohibited them from working at night. Some of the laws also prevented women from being hired for particular jobs. Women were banned from selling liquor and working in bars. They were not allowed to deliver mail. They could not work in mines. They could not operate elevators. Other laws attempted to provide women with better working conditions. They were allowed to sit while working and to have rest periods. Improvements in lighting and ventilation were also part of the protective legislation passed for women workers.

While protective legislation improved the conditions of employment for many women in the early twentieth century, it also limited their employment opportunities, often keeping them from the higher-paying jobs. Night work, for example, always commanded higher wages than day work, even if the jobs were the same.

The Women's Liberation Movement made employment rights a major issue in the 1960's. Groups in the movement pressured Congress to pass laws that would provide equal opportunity for women in employment. Most of the gains in the rights of women on the job have occurred as a result of new federal legislation. These laws attempt to deal with issues of sex discrimination in the workplace.

The Equal Pay Act

In 1963, Congress passed the Equal Pay Act, the first national legislation on women's employment since the 1920's. This law requires that men and women be paid the same wages when they perform jobs that require equal skill, effort, and responsibility and are carried out under similar working conditions. In some situations, however, men and women can be paid different wages for the same job if the wages are based on seniority, on a system of merit, or on a system that bases wages on quantity or quality of production.

The Male-Female Wage Gap: Average Weekly Full-Time Earnings, Wage and Salary Workers, by Sex

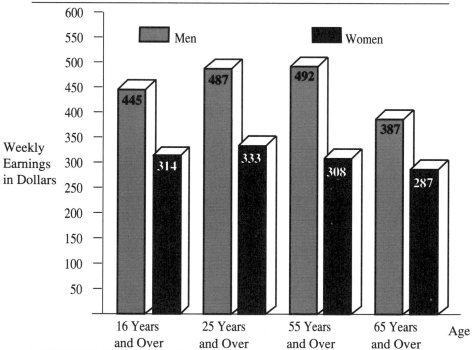

SOURCE: Data are from U.S. Department of Labor, Bureau of Labor Statistics, *News* (August, 1988).

In the 1970's, women attempted to address issues of equal pay in another way. They brought court cases against employers on issues of *comparable worth*. Comparable worth is intended to address the problem that work performed by women is undervalued and underpaid. Pay based on comparable worth, also known as "sex equity," would give women wages equal to those of men for work that is comparable in value to the employer. Comparable worth cases brought by women at the state level in the mid-1980's were relatively successful, but Presidents Reagan and Bush opposed comparable worth, and little was done to develop this concept during their administrations.

Title VII: The 1964 Civil Rights Act

The 1964 Civil Rights Act is another important law which improved women's employment rights. Title VII of this act prohibits discrimination in hiring or on the job based on race, color, religion, national origin, or sex. The category of sex was added to this legislation by a Virginia congressman, who hoped that this added condition would prevent the law from being passed. However, Congresswoman Martha Griffiths (Michigan) fought for the legislation, and the category of sex remained in the final wording of the law.

Title VII established the Equal Employment Opportunity Commission (EEOC) as an agency of the federal government which settles cases of discrimination against women in the workplace. The EEOC is supposed to make sure that women, as well as other groups, enjoy equal opportunities for employment in both the public and private sectors. In 1972, the Equal Employment Opportunity Act was passed. This law gave the EEOC greater authority over employment discrimination, even allowing it to bring some cases to court for settlement.

The EEOC devised guidelines on discrimination with regard to sex, describing employment practices that are discriminatory and, therefore, illegal. These guidelines eliminated or challenged much of the protective state legislation of the past. They required employers who advertised for a man or a woman employee to prove that being male or female was an absolute necessity for a particular job. The guidelines specifically noted that some of the protective legislation — such as the laws that limited women from working at night or from working more than aa limited number of hours per day or from doing certain kinds of work, such as mining or bartending — were illegal.

In its earlier days, the EEOC was relatively successful in providing women with employment discrimination protection. In 1973, for example, the EEOC won a settlement against American Telegraph & Telephone (AT&T), a major employer of women. However, in the 1980's and 1990's, staffing and funding for the EEOC were cut, making it more difficult for women to achieve equal opportunity in employment.

Woman road-crew worker. (Jim Olive/Uniphoto)

Affirmative Action

In the 1960's, the federal government also attempted to prevent employment discrimination by creating a series of regulations that banned employment discrimination by businesses or institutions that received federal contracts or federal funding. Such groups included state governments, public schools and colleges, and private industries, such as some aerospace companies, which had government contracts. These groups were told that they were not to discriminate in the present or future. They also were to make up for past employment discrimination by recruiting, hiring, and promoting minority group members. The original federal affirmative action executive order in 1964 applied to race, color, religion, and national origin. Women were added as a protected group in 1968.

Affirmative action may have had the positive effect of opening some job areas to women. The success of affirmative action programs seems, however, to depend more on the willingness of institutions and businesses to hire additional women than it does on the government's penalizing them if they do not hire women. Few employers have actually had government funds withheld for not complying with affirmative action plans.

During the Reagan and Bush administrations, each president made clear his opposition to affirmative action as a way of eliminating employment discrimination against women and minorities. Reagan revoked many procedures developed for the Office of Federal Contract Compliance Programs (OFCCP), the office that oversees affirmative action. As a result, the OFCCP found it difficult to enforce affirmative action plans. Both Reagan and Bush stated that only voluntary affirmative action programs were needed to protect women and minority workers. These actions made it clear that the presidents would not direct government workers to look carefully at violations of affirmative action policies that had previously been established.

Congress reaffirmed its commitment to affirmative action in the 1980's and 1990's, reviewing and revising existing civil rights legislation, which includes clauses on affirmative action. Sometimes, as in 1988, Congress passed this legislation over the veto of the president. Ironically, however, Congress itself is not required to follow affirmative action policies in employment of individuals who work in congressional offices.

The Pregnancy Discrimination Act

In the past, women have often had to quit their jobs if they become pregnant. If they did not voluntarily quit, the employer could fire them. In 1972, the Equal Employment Opportunity Commission's guidelines established that women who became pregnant while employed cannot be fired or forced to quit their jobs. The pregnancy must be treated as a temporary disability.

The Pregnancy Discrimination Act was passed by Congress in 1978. This law prohibited employers from revoking the rights or benefits of pregnant women within the workplace because of pregnancy. Thanks to this law, pregnant working women have the right to unpaid leaves of absence during pregnancy and childbirth. They can then return to their former jobs or an equivalent job.

The Pregnancy Discrimination Act is one of the few laws since World War II that can be classified as protective legislation. Today, some states are passing family leave legislation that allows either men or women to take a leave of absence when they have a new child. These laws truly do not discriminate on the basis of sex.

Progress in Women's Employment Rights

Generally speaking, women have made substantial progress in gaining access to jobs formerly reserved for men. In the twenty years between 1970 and 1990, women doubled or tripled their percentages in some professions: as lawyers, doctors, architects, engineers, and computer analysts, for example. Other traditional women's occupations, such as nursing and elementary school teaching, are gradually being entered by more men.

It was hoped that the Equal Pay Act would narrow the gap between men's and women's wages. However, this gap is still very apparent. In 1990, white women earned 70 cents for every dollar earned by white men. African-American women earned 62 cents for every dollar earned by white men. Hispanic and Native American women received even lower wages than black women. In terms of equal wages, women still have a long way to go before they achieve equality with men.

Today, women aircraft pilots are no longer rare. (U.S. Department of Defense)

Chapter Eight

Women Who Made a Difference

While few women have reached top political positions in either the United States or Canada, a number of countries have placed women in the top political office. The first woman to become a prime minister was Sirimavo Bandaranaike of Sri Lanka in 1960. A host of other world leaders would follow: Indira Gandhi of India, Golda Meir of Israel, Isabel Perón of Argentina, Margaret Thatcher of Great Britain, Gro Harlem Brundtland of Norway, and Corazon Aquino of the Philippines. Some equally inspiring women are discussed in this chapter.

Sojourner Truth

Sojourner Truth began life sometime around 1797 as a slave named Isabella in Ulster County in the state of New York. She was bought and sold before New York State freed slaves in 1827. Nearly six feet tall and wearing a white turban, she had a regal appearance, a rich voice, and a strong set of opinions that foreshadowed her future.

In 1843, Isabella changed her name to Sojourner Truth. She began to travel the country as a preacher. Wherever she appeared, large groups of people gathered to hear her speak. Because of her oratorical skills, Sojourner Truth was soon invited to address meetings held by the Abolitionists, who were attempting to free slaves throughout the United States. Many of the leaders in the Abolitionist Movement, such as

Lucretia Mott and her husband, were also active in the Women's Rights Movement, and they encouraged Sojourner Truth to speak at women's rights meetings as well.

In 1851, Sojourner Truth delivered what was to become her most famous speech at the 1851 Women's Rights Convention in Akron, Ohio. In it, she said:

> If the first woman God ever made was strong enough to turn the world upside down all alone, these women together ought to be able to turn it back, and get it right side up again! And now [that] they are asking to do it, the men better let them.

The audience cheered loudly at the conclusion of her speech. She had reminded white women and men that they needed to remember that women of all colors, especially women who were still slaves, had a contribution to make and needed rights. The first of these was the right to freedom.

Sojourner Truth exemplifies the kind of women who have helped to reshape the ideas of themselves and others. She was an ordinary woman with an extraordinary gift for public speaking. Throughout her life, she worked to further Christianity, the rights of black people, and the rights of women.

Susan B. Anthony

Susan B. Anthony was born in 1820 in South Adams, Massachusetts, although she lived much of her life in Rochester, New York. Anthony went to schools run by the Quakers and became a schoolteacher. She had taught for about ten years before she became active in the nineteenth-century Women's Rights Movement. In 1851, she met Elizabeth Cady Stanton, who was already a prominent suffragist. For the rest of her life, Anthony would work for women's rights.

Like Sojourner Truth, Susan B. Anthony was active in the Abolitionist Movement as well as the Women's Rights Movement. Her skills included speaking and organizing. She

Susan B. Anthony. (Library of Congress)

traveled the country giving speeches to try to persuade men and women to lobby for women's right to vote. With her friend Stanton, she established the National Woman Suffrage Association (NWSA). In 1890, it was Anthony's skill in organizing that led to the consolidation of the NWSA and the American Woman Suffrage Association (AWSA) as the National American Woman Suffrage Association (NAWSA). She served as the president of the new organization from 1892 until 1900, when she retired at the age of eighty.

Anthony died before the Nineteenth Amendment to the Constitution, which gave women the vote, was ratified. Nevertheless, that amendment is often referred to as the Anthony Amendment. Her contributions to women's rights in the United States were remembered when the United States government minted a one-dollar coin with her picture on it.

Shirley Chisholm

In 1968, Shirley Chisholm became the first African-American woman elected to serve in the U.S. Congress. Few people might have expected that this woman, who had been born in Brooklyn in 1924 to immigrants from the West Indies, would achieve so much in the world of politics.

Chisholm spent several of her younger years with her grandparents in Barbados, but she returned to Brooklyn when she was eleven. She won a scholarship in high school which enabled her to attend Brooklyn College, where she majored in elementary education. She went on to Columbia University to receive a master's degree in elementary education. She worked as a nursery school teacher, as director of a day-care center, and as the director of a school before running for political office.

Chisholm was active in the politics of the Bedford-Stuyvesant area of New York City, where she lived. She served as a state legislator, representing this district from 1965 to 1968. As a state legislator, Chisholm sponsored legislation helpful to both blacks and women, including the introduction of laws to establish publicly funded day-care centers. In 1968, Shirley Chisholm ran for Congress, defeating her opponent, James Farmer, a prominent black man in the Civil Rights Movement, by a three-to-one margin. Chisholm served her district in Congress from 1969 until 1982, when she retired.

In 1972, Shirley Chisholm surprised the nation when she announced that she would campaign for the presidency of the United States. She said that she was running because she wanted "to repudiate the ridiculous notion that the American people will not vote for a qualified candidate simply because he is not white or because she is not a male." She participated in primary elections in many states. While she was unable to win any of the primaries, her candidacy was a first: It focused serious attention on women's issues and the issues of minority

Shirley Chisholm. (Library of Congress)

groups from both the Democratic and Republican parties.

Like Sojourner Truth, Shirley Chisholm became a dynamic and rousing speaker. She is another example of a woman whose life has been devoted to her local community, the state, and the nation and to passing laws that will aid women and minority groups. Her willingness to seek elected political positions for which women were often reluctant to run and her success in attaining these positions have inspired many women to seek public office.

Sandra Day O'Connor

In October, 1981, Sandra Day O'Connor became the first woman Supreme Court justice in the history of the United States when the Senate confirmed her appointment by President Ronald Reagan.

Sandra Day O'Connor was born in El Paso, Texas, and attended elementary and high school there before going to Stanford University. She was an excellent student and completed her degree in three years. She stayed at Stanford to get a law degree in only two more years, graduating third in her class. However, she got her law degree at a time when few private firms hired women as lawyers. One firm offered her a position as a legal secretary, but she refused to accept the job. Instead, she became a county attorney in San Mateo, California.

Before becoming a Supreme Court justice, Sandra Day O'Connor served in several state government positions in Arizona. She was a state senator, an assistant attorney general, a judge for the Arizona Superior Court, and a judge on the Arizona State Court of Appeals. As an Arizona senator, O'Connor earned a reputation for advancing the concerns of women. She supported both a state and a federal equal rights amendment. She sponsored legislation that redefined the community property laws of Arizona and a state "protective" law that ensured women an eight-hour workday.

Her appointment to the Supreme Court opened the highest judicial position in the United States to women. For the first time in U.S. history, a woman's voice was heard when the Supreme Court discussed and decided on women's issues. Her appointment also set an important precedent: It is now unlikely that the Court will ever be without a woman justice in the future.

Indira Gandhi

Indira Gandhi was the first woman to serve as prime minister of India. She was chosen as prime minister in 1966 and served until 1977. In 1980, she returned to office and served until she was murdered in 1984 by two men in her own security forces.

Indira Gandhi does not represent the norm for women in India. Few women have served in the government or in India's parliament. It is unlikely that she would have gained her position had she not been the daughter of Jawaharlal Nehru, who had been the first prime minister of the newly independent nation of India (1947-1964). As early as 1955, she became a member of the Congress Party, the dominant political party in India.

While Indira Gandhi was prime minister, many legal rights were extended to women, particularly in the area of reproductive rights. The Indian government supports and subsidizes family planning because it is concerned with slowing the growth of its population, which is increasing faster than food production. Consequently, many people in India have difficulty getting enough food to survive. In addition to making contraception available and free, the government since 1975 has supported abortion through the twentieth week of pregnancy for women who want it. Women who seek abortions do not need the permission of their husbands.

The most controversial reproductive rights policy pursued by the Indian government under Indira Gandhi was sterilization. Both men and women could receive money if either agreed to be sterilized. Gandhi's government particularly tried to persuade poor men and women in the countryside to be sterilized. Critics of these policies believed that the consequences of sterilization were not fully explained to these people.

Gandhi found ways to be an effective political leader and refused to be merely a puppet manipulated by male advisers. It may be many years before another woman serves as prime minister of India, but because of Indira Gandhi, women may be more willing to tackle the job of top political leader in nations where men have been especially dominant in society.

Margaret Thatcher

In 1979, Margaret Thatcher became the first woman prime minister in the history of Great Britain and Europe. In parliamentary governments, the prime minister's position is as important as that of the president in the United States. She stayed in that position until the end of 1990.

Like Indira Gandhi, Thatcher became interested in politics at a fairly early age. She first ran for a parliamentary seat in 1950, when she was only twenty-five years old. She lost that election, but she kept running until she finally won a seat in 1959. In the meantime, in 1954, she had also become a barrister (the British term for "lawyer").

During the 1970's, Thatcher served in a number of important ministry and cabinet positions whenever the Conservative Party was in power. By 1975, she was the leader of the Conservative Party, which meant that when that party took over Parliament in 1979, she became the prime minister. Thatcher's policies as prime minister did not generally improve the condition of women in Great Britain. In fact, many of her policies increased unemployment and hurt both women and men economically. Nonetheless, she was extremely popular with the British voters until shortly before her retirement.

Thatcher is another model for women who aspire to political leadership. One of the reasons that men (and some women) have given for not wanting to see women in key leadership roles is their fear that women would not be able to react to crises as well as men. In particular, there is a fear that women would be less willing to go to war if such a move were necessary. Many people liked Thatcher because she proved that, in the face of crisis, women could be as tough and capable as men. In 1982, for example, she led Great Britain in a short war with Argentina over the Falkland Islands. This enhanced her popularity and put to rest the idea that women political leaders are unwilling to make tough decisions.

Aung San Suu Kyi

Aung San Suu Kyi, born in Rangoon on June 19, 1945, is the leader of the National League for Democracy in Myanmar (formerly Burma). Since July of 1989, she has been detained by the ruling military junta, which has kept her under house arrest, separated from both her family and her friends. Although the National League for Democracy overwhelmingly won victory in the national elections in May, 1990, the military government has refused to release her or to allow the National League for Democracy to take office. Essentially, although Aung San Suu Kyi has been elected to power, she has been unable to assume her position as Myanmar's prime minister.

Despite these obstacles, Suu Kyi achieved national and international recognition. In 1990, she received the Sakharov Prize for the freedom of thought, and in 1991, she received the Nobel Peace Prize for her willingness to struggle for democracy and human rights, including those of women. Aung San Suu Kyi is an inspiration to women who aspire to be political leaders and a reminder that women may face great difficulties — even life-threatening ones — in that role.

Ella DeRouselle, a sixth-grade teacher, takes a break from grading assignments; primary and secondary educators have traditionally been women, these women have had a huge influence on many young lives. (U.S. Department of Defense)

Chapter Nine

International Women's Rights

The women's rights issues that have been examined throughout this book are issues that women around the world are facing. The way that these rights have been addressed, country by country, depends on the cultural, religious, historical, and economic background of each nation. Just as women have had to organize in the United States and Canada to get legislation and amendments passed to obtain legal rights, women in other countries have sought protection for women's rights through law.

Many of the nations of the world provide *de jure* ("by law") protection for women's rights. Whether these laws also protect women *de facto* ("in fact") is less clear. However, the passage of legislation is certainly a start in the struggle to achieve these rights, as history in the United States has made clear. Usually, a law must be in place for many years before it has a significant effect.

Internationally, women's rights have been fostered in several ways. One way has been to seek international agreements that encourage all nations to pass laws that promote women's rights in their own countries.

The Role of the United Nations

Since the United Nations was created in 1945, it has been a leading agency for the promotion of women's rights in all countries. The charter that established the United Nations called for universal respect for and observance of human rights and fundamental freedoms for all people, regardless of race, sex, language, or religion. One of the first declarations passed by the United Nations upon its creation in 1948 was the Universal Declaration of Human Rights, which defines basic human rights in a long list of freedoms and protections, including equality under the law. The United Nations reaffirmed that human rights belong to all people and that women cannot be discriminated against with regard to these basic rights. Countries that are members of the United Nations, therefore, must accept the legal and moral responsibilities for eliminating inequalities between men and women.

In subsequent declarations, the United Nations has also addressed many key women's rights. In 1952, the Convention on the Political Rights of Women was passed. By 1987, ninety-four nations had ratified this agreement, accepting their obligation to secure for women the right to hold political office.

Other U.N. agreements call for an end to discrimination against women in education and in employment. Women's rights in marriage are addressed in a number of agreements, including the Convention on Consent to Marriage, Minimum Age for Marriage, and Registration of Marriage, passed in 1962. This document calls for each nation to pass legislation to ensure that men and women are equal partners in marriage. Because women in many countries have frequently been "married off" by their parents at a young age and without their consent, a minimum age of marriage is to be established by each country. Nations are encouraged to repeal laws and discourage customs that allow girls to be married while they are still children.

Recognizing that women in many countries had not been granted the rights that the U.N. agreements had attempted to secure for them over the years, a new treaty affirming international commitment to eradicating discrimination against women was passed in 1979. The Convention on the Elimination of All Forms of Discrimination Against Women reiterated that women should not be discriminated against in employment, education, and political participation. It also recognized the need for both men and women to take responsibility for rearing children and urged countries to provide child care, since both parents often work outside the home.

The unique problems of worldwide discrimination against women also led the United Nations to announce the "Decade for Women: Equality, Development, and Peace," from 1975 through 1985. The decade was intended to focus international concern on the issues of gender equality. The Decade for Women began with the International Women's Year in 1975,

---

The United Nations Declaration of the Rights of Women

Article 1.   Discrimination against women, denying or limiting as it does their equality or rights with men, is fundamentally unjust and constitutes an offence against human dignity.

Article 2.   All appropriate measures shall be taken to abolish existing laws, customs, regulations and practices which are discriminatory against women, and to establish adequate legal protection for equal rights of men and women. . . .

Article 4.   All appropriate measures shall be taken to ensure to women on equal terms with, without discrimination:
(a)   the right to vote in elections and be eligible for election to all publicly elected bodies;
(b)   the right to vote in all public referenda;
(c)   the right to hold public office and to exercise all public functions.
Such rights should be guaranteed by legislation.

---

culminating in the World Conference on Women, held in Mexico City during the summer of that year. The conference was attended by representatives of 133 countries, including Canada and the United States. Delegates discussed the status of women in nations around the world and examined the major obstacles to equality for women. One task that the conference set for itself was to establish a World Plan of Action for the decade.

In 1980, a second World Conference on Women was held in Copenhagen, Denmark, to review the progress that had been made in achieving the World Plan of Action at the decade's halfway point. Then, in 1985, a Third World Conference was held in Nairobi, Kenya, to appraise the achievements of the United Nations Decade for Women. In the latter conference, 157 governments participated. For two weeks they evaluated these achievements in terms of peace, equality, and development. In the area of equality, most countries had made significant progress in passing laws to give women full legal and civil rights. The greatest advances had occurred in nations that were most economically and politically developed. In nations where economic and political systems were still developing, women continued to play more traditional roles and to enjoy less political and legal acceptance.

The Third World Conference also highlighted women's roles in the economic development of their nations. The participants noted that it was often difficult to get statistics that adequately measured women's contributions to economic development, although in every developing nation women played a significant role in the production of food. Discrimination against women in employment opportunities — in both the types of jobs available to them and the wages that were paid to them — were problems in all countries. An additional burden, which seemed to be universal, was the notion that women should do the majority of housework and child care, even when they were also employed outside the home.

Perhaps one of the most important results of the U.N. Decade for Women was that it changed attitudes: The conferences held during the United Nations Decade for Women often provided women from different countries with their first opportunities to meet with women of other nations and cultures, and to recognize the similarities between and differences in their problems. Many of the women who served as delegates returned to their home countries with renewed energy to struggle for women's rights.

The international focus on women's rights in the 1970's and 1980's helped women in a number of countries achieve more rights, at least legally. Nonetheless, there is still significant variation in women's rights from country to country. A quick look at several nations points out this variation.

Canada

While Canadian women, like U.S. women, have political rights, only a small percentage have been selected for political office. About 7 percent of the seats in Parliament are currently held by women. Two women have been chosen to serve on the Canadian Supreme Court. Some women also serve in cabinet positions.

In 1984, Jeanne Sauve became the first woman governor-general of Canada. She was appointed to this post because of her twelve years of service in Parliament, including her work as Speaker of the House of Commons. The governor-general is the head of state, representing the entire country. Appointed rather than elected, the governor-general is responsible for summoning and dissolving Canada's parliament. She has the right to authorize treaties, receive and send ambassadors, and give royal assent to bills passed by the House of Commons and the Senate. Whatever the governor-general does, she must have the approval of other ministers in the Canadian government. While the office is primarily symbolic and most power lies with the prime minister and Parliament, the governor-general's position is important in Canadian history.

While Canada's 1977 Human Rights Act legally protects women against discrimination in employment and gives them the right to equal pay for equal work, many women work in minimum-wage jobs or work part-time and therefore receive wages that are lower than those of men. They also continue to be disproportionately represented in traditional women's jobs, such as secretarial and sales positions.

In the area of reproductive rights, Canadian women still have difficulty obtaining information on birth control and contraceptives. Provinces cannot ban the use of contraceptives, but they do not have to make information on contraceptives available. In some provinces, contraceptives are impossible to buy. Abortion is available when a woman's life or health is endangered, but it must be performed in a hospital, and hospitals do not have to provide abortions. Like the U.S. government, the Canadian government has cut funding of family planning clinics, thus limiting women's access to information.

Sweden

Studies have found that Sweden guarantees women the most rights. Swedish women have had the right to vote since 1919, and about 30 percent of the members of the Swedish legislature, the Riksdag, are women. Women have also been appointed to the Swedish Supreme Court.

The Swedish constitution ensures full equality between men and women. A 1980 law bans discrimination against women in employment. Men in Sweden have equal responsibility for child care and housework, and the majority of Swedish women are employed outside the home.

Swedish men and women have had access to contraceptives since 1938. Family planning is encouraged, and abortion requires only the consent of the mother through the first eighteen weeks of pregnancy. Thus, Swedish women have extensive reproductive rights.

Marriage and divorce in Sweden require the consent of both men and women. A couple can voluntarily dissolve the marriage if both desire to do so. Child custody may be joint or with a single parent, depending on what is in the best interests of the child.

Brazil

Brazil is a large Latin American country with a growing population. In Brazil, women have had voting rights since 1932, but few women have been elected to political office.

Since 1962, Brazil's constitution has had an equal rights amendment, and in 1976, an equal pay act was passed. However, women work primarily in traditional women's occupations in agriculture, child care, and education — largely because traditional values of family and marriage remain strong in Brazil. This is evident in the country's policies on marriage, divorce, and reproductive rights. Brazilian women take the names of their husbands, and the Marriage Law states that the husband is the legal head of the marriage. Divorce was legalized in 1977, but couples must be separated for three to five years before they can be divorced. Information on family planning and access to birth control are still not widespread. Abortion is available only when a mother's life is threatened.

While Brazilian women have gained some rights in the last twenty years, women's organizations are still fighting to achieve others.

China

Chinese women achieved many rights during the second half of the twentieth century. They were granted full political rights in 1949. Equal rights for women were also guaranteed in the 1952 and the 1982 constitutions. Approximately 20 percent of the People's Congress (China's legislature) are women. The majority of women work outside the home in agriculture and industry. One-third of all the scientists in China are women— an indication of how the Chinese are encouraging women to pursue both traditional and nontraditional occupations. There is also equal pay for equal work.

Since overpopulation is a problem for much of China, the government has introduced a number of policies that encourage couples to do family planning. Women must be at least twenty years old to marry, and men must be twenty-two. Contraceptives and abortion are legal and free. The government, facing an enormous and growing population, has encouraged the use of birth control since 1955. Each couple is supposed to have only one child. This policy is quite controversial and may lead women in China, at some point, to insist that they need to have more rights to reproduce, rather than more choice over not having children.

Japan

Economically, Japan is a modern industrial society where women have many rights by law. In practice, however, Japanese women have fewer rights than are legally guaranteed to them, partly because of a culture that has emphasized the subservience of women for many years. The Japanese constitution of 1947 gives women the right to vote and contains an equal rights amendment. Nevertheless, fewer than 10 percent of the members of the Japanese parliament are women.

Marriage is also defined in Japan's constitution as requiring the mutual consent of both men and women. Women can marry at age sixteen, while men must be eighteen. Married people can take either the husband's or the wife's name. Both the husband and wife are jointly responsible for the debts and expenses of the household.

United Nations' International Women's Year. (Library of Congress)

The employment rights of women, particularly those who work in agriculture or part-time in industry, are still not well protected. Japanese women have limited control over their ability to reproduce. Abortion is available if the health or economic security of a woman is threatened, but the husband must agree to the abortion. Some contraceptives are available, while others are banned.

Although Japanese women have had limited rights, the growing shortage of Japanese workers may lead to more rights for women. If the Japanese choose to encourage women to become more fully involved in the economic sector, women will probably agitate for additional rights.

Kenya

Women in Kenya have a variety of ethnic and religious backgrounds. They received voting rights as well as equal rights in the constitution of 1963, but few women are actively involved in politics. The majority of women in Kenya work in agriculture or in the home and do not receive compensation for their labor. There is no equal-pay policy. The marriage and divorce laws are varied and complex. Separate laws for the different religious groups often make it easier for men than women to get a divorce. Contraception is available but not widely used, and abortions are available only to protect the life of the mother.

The problems of women in Kenya are similar to those of women in many developing countries. Women have political rights but are kept in very traditional roles. In the years since the United Nations was founded, women's rights have become more important than ever before in history. The international legal agreements that the United Nations has established and the international women's conferences have helped women begin to address their need for equality now. If the next decades are to see substantial gains, however, women must continue to make their voices heard.

Chapter Ten

Outlook for the Future

Women have made many strides toward gaining basic human rights. Moreover, they have organized nationally and internationally to address issues of special concern to women. Much of this progress has been in the area of attitudes and beliefs: At this point in time, the percentage of men and women who believe that women should be treated equally with men is great enough that issues of particular concern to women will undoubtedly continue to be significant in many countries.

Political Rights

Nevertheless, women are still far from being full participants in the political systems of most countries, although in many, they have achieved the legal right to vote and to run for political office. Cultural ideas about appropriate roles for men and women still seem to militate against women serving as government officials, whether in the United States, Argentina, or China. The lack of women government officials makes it difficult for issues of concern to women to get the full attention they deserve.

The Equal Rights Amendment

In the United States, one long-standing issue in political rights will resurface in the decades ahead: whether there is a need for the national Equal Rights Amendment. The U.N. declarations on women's political rights mandate equal rights laws or amendments, and many nations have added such laws

to their constitutions. In 1977, Canada passed the Human
Rights Act, which includes equal rights for women. The
United States, on the other hand, defeated the Equal Rights
Amendment (ERA) in 1982.

In 1923, Alice Paul, leader of the National Woman's Party,
proposed the first equal rights amendment, which stated:

> Men and women shall have equal rights throughout the United
> States and every place to [that is, within] its jurisdiction.

This amendment would have given women equal rights in
local, state, and national laws.

Alice Paul's equal rights amendment never received the
approval of Congress, although it was presented each year for
approval. It was opposed by both men and women, even
women who had fought for voting rights. These critics
believed that existing legislation, which provided special
protections for women, would be nullified if an equal rights
amendment were passed. They believed that women's rights
were better protected by special legislation rather than by a law
guaranteeing equal treatment.

It was not until the National Organization for Women, the
major women's advocacy group in the United States, endorsed
the idea of an ERA in 1967 that there was national sentiment
in favor of an amendment. In 1972, Congress approved an
equal rights amendment sponsored by members of the House
of Representatives, including Michigan's Martha Griffiths and
California's Yvonne Braithwaite-Burke. The language of the
congressionally approved amendment was somewhat different
from the amendment proposed by Alice Paul, but it was
referred to as the Alice Paul Amendment nevertheless.

In quick order, thirty of the thirty-eight states needed to
ratify the amendment so it could become part of the
Constitution did so. Then, the amendment ran into difficulty.
Among the states that did not ratify the ERA were Alabama,

Arizona, Arkansas, Florida, Georgia, Illinois, Louisiana, Mississippi, Nevada, North Carolina, Utah, and Virginia. The majority of these states are Southern states or states that have large conservative populations.

Most of these states allowed the issue of ratification to be decided by state legislatures rather than placing the question on the ballot so that all the people could vote on it. These state legislatures were particularly dominated by male legislators opposed to the ERA. By the time of the deadline for passage, 1979, three more states were still needed. Congress decided to extend the deadline for passage until 1982, but the additional time did not help. The ERA died in 1982.

The ERA also failed because the groups opposed to it — such as the STOP ERA organization, led by Phyllis Schlafly — were more effective in persuading these legislators of their

Women working together to secure their rights — now and for the future. (Michael J. Pettypool/Uniphoto)

views. These groups argued that the ERA would abolish the natural differences between men and women, that the ERA would require women to be drafted into the army and force them into military combat, that the ERA would make separate public lavatories illegal, and that much of the existing legislation that protected women would be annulled. These arguments played on the fears that many men, and even some women, harbored: that women were making too many demands, too soon, for equality.

In 1989, the ERA was again introduced into Congress, but as of 1992 it had not passed. However, poll data indicate that about 65 percent of the U.S. population favors the passage of such an amendment. Consequently, it will continue to be brought up until it passes. As more women move into state legislatures and Congress, additional support for the amendment will arise.

Economic Rights

Another major area of concern for women in all countries is economic rights. Women everywhere are attempting to gain the ability to care for themselves and their families economically. In some countries, this means equality in education. In many countries, fewer women than men receive high school and college educations. Yet it is only through obtaining advanced degrees that women can become doctors, teachers, lawyers, and business managers — the higher-paying jobs.

In most countries, women are struggling to receive equal pay for equal or comparable work. Additionally, they need adequate child care when one or both parents are working outside the home. Each country is going to have to address issues of child care, education, and comparable pay for women.

Sexual Harassment

Women who are employed continue to face sexual harassment. Sexual harassment is usually defined as deliberate or repeated verbal remarks, gestures, or physical contact of a sexual nature that are unwelcomed by the recipient.

In 1980, the Equal Employment Opportunity Commission issued guidelines on sexual harassment, stating that it was a form of sexual discrimination in employment and was illegal. The guidelines recognize two different forms of sexual harassment: one in which the employee is made to believe that she or he will receive economic benefits only by agreeing to give her employer sexual favors; and a second type in which the employer creates a hostile working environment for the employee by continually making sexual remarks, even though he or she never demands explicit sexual favors.

In 1991, sexual harassment became a topic of public discussion across the United States when Clarence Thomas, President Bush's nominee for a Supreme Court position, was accused of sexual harassment by one of his former employees, lawyer Anita Hill. Many people in the United States watched their televisions as Hill and Thomas appeared before the Senate Judiciary Committee. Hill charged that Thomas had sexually harassed her when he was in charge of the Equal Employment Opportunity Commission — a position in which he was responsible, among other things, for protecting women against sexual harassment by their employers. Hill had worked for Thomas during this time.

Many people found it difficult to understand why Hill had continued to work for Thomas if she had, in fact, been harassed. Experts in the area of sexual harassment, however, found her testimony credible and typical of the experience of other women who have been sexually harassed. Nevertheless, after the hearings, the majority of the Senate believed that Thomas had not harassed Anita Hill, so Thomas was confirmed as a Supreme Court justice.

Despite this decision, the widespread media coverage of the Senate hearings focused much-needed public attention on

Reproductive rights means control, choice, and *responsibility; women caring for the health and welfare of their children and pursuing their own interests and happiness.* (William Kurnizki)

sexual harassment and made people more aware of the complexities of harassment issues and how common it is for women — and a growing number of men — to experience this type of abuse.

Reproductive Rights in the Future

In the 1970's and the early 1980's, the U.S. federal government provided financing for family planning clinics across the nation. These clinics provided information on birth control, pregnancy testing at very low cost, family counseling, and prescriptions for some forms of contraception such as birth control pills. In the 1980's and 1990's, during the administrations of Presidents Ronald Reagan and George Bush, the funding for family planning was severely cut, making it much more difficult for women in the United States to obtain information and services on women's reproductive rights. Simultaneously, federal government agencies, the Supreme Court, and some of the state legislatures were also making decisions that threatened to make it difficult for women to retain the rights they had won in the 1970's.

A disturbing development during the late 1980's and the 1990's — the physical obstruction of medical clinics that perform abortions and the intimidation of doctors and family members by radical pro-life activists — has begun to remove access to abortions from women trying to exercise their legal right to choose. Peaceful demonstrations have sometimes turned into violent confrontations. Those on both sides of the issue are concerned about the dangers of allowing civil disobedience to push people beyond the law.

In the United States and other countries, the future will undoubtedly see additional discussion of whether abortion should be one method women can use to control reproduction. The Supreme Court of the United States has been hearing cases involving women's right to abortion since its landmark decision in *Roe v. Wade* in 1973. Since then, however, new justices appointed to the Supreme Court have indicated some opposition to this right. In their most recent decisions, they have given the states more authority to decide whether, and under what conditions, to allow abortions. If they continue this trend, laws across the states could again become very restrictive with regard to abortion.

Women may have to organize more effectively in each state to safeguard their reproductive rights. Another key to reproductive rights is education: As women become more aware of the existence of different forms of contraception — and thus the possibility of controlling their pregnancies — they will be more likely to demand access to contraceptives and hence reproductive freedom.

A World for Women?

All nations, including the United States and Canada, must expand women's rights if women are to be equal and full participants in every aspect of life. While much has been achieved, much remains to be done — from political and economic rights to reproductive rights and simple respect. Changes will be, as they have been in the past, gradual. Furthermore, they will vary from country to country, depending on the nation's economic stability, its cultural institutions, and the traditional roles played by women.

One thing is certain, however: The world of the future will be one in which human beings of all races, creeds, *and* genders will be more interdependent than ever before. As the world economy and the need to protect our common "nation" — Mother Earth — become more critical, the challenge of respecting women's rights, and all human rights, will become more urgent.

Time Line

1776   The United States publishes its Declaration of Independence.

1776   Women gain the right to vote in some parts of New Jersey.

1787   The United States Constitution is ratified.

1807   Women in New Jersey lose the right to vote.

1839   Mississippi passes the first Married Women's Property Act.

1848   The first women's rights convention is held in Seneca Falls, New York, and issues the Declaration of Sentiments.

1851   Sojourner Truth, a former slave, speaks about the similarities between the struggle to abolish slavery and the struggle for women's rights at a women's rights convention in Akron, Ohio.

1866   Elizabeth Cady Stanton runs for Congress but does not win.

1869   The National Woman Suffrage Association (NWSA) and the American Woman Suffrage Association (AWSA) are founded.

1870   Women get the right to vote and serve on juries in the territory of Wyoming.

1872   Women, among them Susan B. Anthony, are arrested for attempting to vote in the presidential election.

1875   In *Minor v. Heppersett*, the Supreme Court decides that women are citizens but do not have the right to vote.

1890   The merger of the NWSA and the AWSA produces the National American Woman Suffrage Association (NAWSA).

1893   New Zealand gives women the right to vote.

1896   The National Association for Colored Women is formed.

1916   The National Woman's Party is founded.

1917   Jeannette Rankin is the first woman elected to Congress.

1918   Euroamerican women are given the right to vote in Canada.

1919   Sweden gives women the right to vote.

1920   The Nineteenth Amendment gives U.S. women voting rights.

1921   The Sheppard-Towner Act, also known as the Maternity and Infancy Act, provides money to states to improve prenatal care and infant care.

1922   The Cable Act establishes individual citizenship for women.

1924   Native American women can vote in the United States.

1940 Quebec gives women the right to vote.

1946 The Japanese pass an equal rights amendment and give women voting rights.

1948 The United Nations issues its Universal Declaration of Human Rights.

1949 China grants women full political rights.

1952 The U.N. Convention on the Political Rights of Women is approved.

1960 Sirimavo Bandaranaike of Sri Lanka becomes the first woman prime minister.

1960 Native American women get the vote in Canada.

1961 John F. Kennedy establishes the first President's Commission on the Status of Women.

1962 The U.N. Convention on Consent to Marriage, Minimum Age for Marriage, and Registration of Marriage is approved.

1962 An equal rights amendment is added to Brazil's constitution.

1963 The U.S. Equal Pay Act is passed.

1964 Title VII of the Civil Rights Act prohibits sex discrimination in employment.

1965 In *Griswold v. Connecticut*, the Supreme Court decides that married women have a right to use contraceptives.

1965 The Voting Rights Act improves black women's voting rights.

1966 The National Organization for Women is established.

1966 Indira Gandhi becomes prime minister of India.

1967 Women's consciousness-raising groups begin to form.

1968 Shirley Chisholm is the first black woman elected to the United States Congress.

1970 In *Taylor v. Louisiana*, the Supreme Court determines that women can serve on juries.

1970 The Voting Rights Act passes; the Twenty-sixth Amendment gives the vote to eighteen-year-olds.

1971 National Women's Political Caucus is founded.

1971 Switzerland gives women the right to vote.

1972 Congress passes the Equal Employment Opportunity Act.

1973 The Supreme Court decides in *Roe v. Wade* that women have the right to an abortion.

1975 The first World Conference on Women takes place in Mexico City.

1975 The Equal Credit Opportunity Act is passed by Congress.

1977 The Human Rights Act gives women in Canada equal rights.

1978 Congress passes the Pregnancy Discrimination Act.

1979 In *Duren v. Missouri*, the Supreme Court determines that laws on jury service must treat men and women the same.

1979 The U.N. Convention on the Elimination of All Forms of Discrimination Against Women is approved.

1979 Margaret Thatcher becomes the first woman prime minister of Great Britain.

1980 The Second World Conference on Women takes place in Copenhagen, Denmark.

1981 Sandra Day O'Connor is appointed as the first woman Supreme Court justice.

1984 Jeanne Sauve becomes the first woman governor-general of Canada.

1985 The Third World Conference on Women is held in Nairobi.

1988 The Women's Business Ownership Act is passed by Congress.

1988 The Women's Agenda Conference takes place in Des Moines, Iowa; women discuss crucial issues such as education, health care, reproductive choice, and child care.

1991 Aung San Suu Kyi, leader of the National League for Democracy in Myanmar (formerly Burma), wins the Nobel Peace Prize.

Publications

Biography

Ferris, Jeri. *Walking the Road to Freedom: A Story About Sojourner Truth.* Minneapolis, Minn.: Lerner Publications, 1989. This biography of Sojourner Truth is primarily for readers in the third to sixth grades. It is only sixty-four pages long but includes the famous "Ain't I a Woman?" speech.

Nadel, Laurie. *Corazon Aquino: Journey to Power.* New York: Julian Messner, 1987. This 121-page biography looks at Corazon Aquino's life before and after she became the president of the Philippines. For grades 5 and up.

Scheader, Catherine. *Shirley Chisholm: Teacher and Congresswoman.* Hillside, N.J.: Enslow, National Women's History Project, 1990. This 128-page biography of Shirley Chisholm, the first black woman to serve in Congress and run for the presidency of the United States, is written for students in grades 5 and up.

Weisberg, Barbara. *Susan Anthony, Woman Suffragist.* New York: Chelsea House, 1988. This biography stresses Anthony's major role in fighting for voting rights for women. It includes photographs of many of the most significant suffragist leaders in the nineteenth-century Women's Rights Movement.

Woods, Harold, and Geraldine Woods. *Equal Justice: A Biography of Sandra Day O'Connor.* New York: Macmillan Children's Group, 1985. Beginning with Sandra Day O'Connor's early life on her parents' ranch, this biography follows her career to the Supreme Court of the United States. Background on other Supreme Court justices is also given.

History

Bingham, Marjorie Wall. *Women and the Constitution: Student Textbook.* Atlanta: The Carter Center of Emory University, 1990. The author looks at different aspects of the constitutional history of women and provides exercises for students. Resource text for teachers.

Fisher, Maxine P. *Women in the Third World.* New York: Franklin Watts, 1989. Designed for students in grades 6 and above, this volume examines the issues that concern women in several Third World countries.

Hoople, Cheryl G. *As I Saw It: Women Who Lived the American Adventure*. New York: Dial Press, 1978. The author collected letters, diaries, journals, interviews, and speeches of women from the earliest days of settlement in North America to the late nineteenth century and weaves them into an interesting account of how women regard American history.

Landau, Elaine. *Hidden Heroines: Women in American History*. New York: Julian Messner, 1975. This book examines the history of women from the beginning of U.S. history to the passage of the Nineteenth Amendment. For grades 4 through 7.

Lerner, Gerda, ed. *Black Women in White America: A Documentary History*. New York: Vintage Books, 1973. The most complete set of documents on the history of African-American women from 1811 to 1970. A good source for important moments in black women's history.

McCullough, Joan. *First of All: Significant "Firsts" by American Women*. New York: Holt, Rinehart and Winston, 1980. This book gives short statements, including names and dates, about women's achievements in the armed services, the arts, politics, aviation, religion, science and medicine, and sports.

Stevenson, Janet. *Women's Rights*. New York: Franklin Watts, 1972. Although this volume is somewhat dated, it discusses the roles of the nineteenth-century Women's Rights Movement and the twentieth century's Women's Liberation Movement in securing women's rights.

Wharton, Mary. *Rights of Women*. New York: Gloucester Press, Aladdin Books, 1989. This sixty-two-page book examines the ways that women throughout the world continue to argue for the need for women's rights in education, politics, work, marriage, and parenting.

Zophy, Angela Howard, ed. *Handbook of American Women's History*. Hamden, Conn.: Garland Reference Library of the Humanities, 1990. An essential compendium of women's history in the United States. Each section is well written; all major organizations, women, and issues are covered.

Media Resources

Videotapes and Filmstrips

Elizabeth Cady Stanton and Susan B. Anthony: Women's Suffrage Leaders. Princeton, N.J.: Films for the Humanities, 1988. A twenty-four-minute videotape that looks at Stanton and Anthony's founding of the National Woman Suffrage Association.

There's No Such Thing as Women's Work. Washington, D.C.: Women's Bureau, Department of Labor, 1991. This videotape examines all the different kinds of work women do, quickly dispelling the notion that there is a limited definition of "women's work."

A Woman's Place. Windsor, Calif.: National Women's History Project, 1975. This video, narrated by actress Julie Harris, is based on material that was gathered for *Life* magazine's special 1975 report, "Remarkable American Women." It is twenty-five minutes long and can be shown to sixth-graders.

Women: An American History. Skokie, Ill.: Encyclopædia Britannica, 1976. A series of six filmstrips and cassettes that deal with major moments in U.S. women's history. Includes segments on the fight for equality and the modern women's movement.

Women in American Life. Windsor, Calif.: National Women's History Project, 1988. A series of five videotapes, between fifteen and twenty-five minutes long, that look at women's lives and their contributions to history from 1861 to 1880, 1880 to 1920, 1917 to 1942, 1942 to 1955, and 1955 to 1977. Good background material.

Audiotapes, Records, and Computer Software

But the Women Rose: Voices of Women in American History. New York: Folkways Records, 1976. A double album of excerpts from women's speeches throughout U.S. history, from 1700 to 1970.

Legacies: A History of Women and the Family in America, 1607-1870. Washington, D.C.: Annenberg/CPB Project, 1987. Sixteen videotapes covering the early moments in women's history.

The Medalists: Women in History. Windsor, Calif.: Hartley Courseware, 1990. Available from the National Women's History Project. A complete software game in the Apple Format. Students identify prominent women of the world from the last two centuries.

The Negro Woman. New York: Folkways Records, 1975. A documentary of the history of African-American women.

Side by Side: Reenactments of Scenes from Women's History, 1848 to 1920. New York: Galaxia Records, 1978. A double album of dramatic readings from women's history.

Songs of the Suffragettes. New York: Folkways Records, 1975. A single album of the songs that women sang as they were fighting for voting rights.

Organizations
and
Hotlines

Mexican American Women's National Association
1101 17th St. NW, Suite 803
Washington, DC 20036
(202) 833-0060
   Founded in 1974, this organization promotes leadership and development
for Mexican-American and other Hispanic women. It is particularly
concerned with pay equity, teenage pregnancy, and children in poverty. The
group sponsors a yearly conference for Hispanic high school girls,
emphasizing self-esteem and career counseling.

National Abortion Rights Action League
1101 14th St. NW, Fifth Floor
Washington, DC 20005
(202) 408-4600
   Founded in 1969 to develop an effective lobby for pro-choice positions,
NARAL coordinates the work of a number of groups that want to keep
abortion legal and available to women.

National Association of Commissions of Women
YWCA Bldg. M-10
624 Ninth St. NW
Washington, DC 20001
(202) 628-5030
   This organization was founded in 1970 and has regional, state, and local
branches, all trying to further the legal, social, political, economic, and
educational quality of the lives of women in the United States. Publishes
informational pamphlets and a newsletter.

National Association of Cuban-American Women of the USA
YWCA Bldg. M-10
624 Ninth St. NW
Washington, DC 20001

This organization, founded in 1972, maintains a large library of works on Cuban and Cuban-American history. It addresses issues of particular concern to Hispanic women, such as equal education and job training, fair immigration laws, and the right to meaningful work with adequate pay.

National Conference of Puerto Rican Women
5 Thomas Circle
Washington, DC 20005
(202) 387-4716

This organization was founded in 1972 to promote the participation of Puerto Rican and other Hispanic women in the economic, political, and social life of the United States and Puerto Rico. It holds an annual convention.

National Organization for Women
1000 16th St. NW, Suite 700
Washington, DC 20036
(202) 331-0066

This largest women's organization in the United States was founded in 1966. NOW seeks to eliminate discrimination against women in every area of women's lives. It also advocates a national equal rights amendment. Its biweekly newspaper focuses on women's issues, including laws up for consideration by Congress.

National Women's History Project
7738 Bell Road
Windsor, CA 95492
(707) 838-6000

A resource clearinghouse for women's history which conducts educational conferences and workshops, publishes a quarterly newsletter, produces videotapes, and coordinates the Women's History Network.

National Women's Political Caucus
1275 K St. NW, Suite 750
Washington, DC 20005
(202) 898-1100

This group, founded in 1971, is multipartisan and is organized at the local, state, and national levels. It raises women's political issues at every level of government and encourages women to run for political office and to vote for candidates who support women's issues.

North American Indian Women's Association
P.O. Box 805
Eagle Butte, SD 57625
Founded in 1970, this organization is composed of Native American women who promote awareness of the Native American cultures and betterment of family life, health, and education — all important issues for both Native American women and Native American men.

Organization of Chinese American Women
1300 N St. NW, Suite 100
Washington, DC 20005
(202) 638-0330
This group was founded in 1977 to advance the concerns of Chinese American Women in the United States. It distributes a newsletter and a quarterly publication.

Organization of Pan Asian American Women
P.O. Box 39218 NW
Washington, DC 20016
(202) 659-9370
Founded in 1976, this organization promotes the interests of Asian Pacific-American women in the United States, encouraging them to get the leadership skills they need. Sponsors a speakers' bureau.

Pro-Life Action League
6160 N. Cicero, No. 600
Chicago, IL 60646
(312) 777-2900
This group, founded in 1980, works to stop abortions through legal and nonviolent means. It sponsors seminars and holds community presentations on pro-life issues.

Third World Women's Project
Institute for Policy Studies
1601 Connecticut Ave. NW, Fifth Floor

Washington, DC 20009
(202) 234-9382

The major purpose of this organization, which was founded in 1981, is to educate the public on women's issues and other human rights issues in Third World countries. It provides access to videotapes and filmstrips related to these issues.

Human Rights

EQUALITY NOW

INDEX